Second Edition

# EVALUATING THE IMPACT OF LEADERSHIP DEVELOPMENT

Second Edition

# EVALUATING THE IMPACT OF LEADERSHIP DEVELOPMENT

Tracy E. Patterson, Sarah Stawiski, Kelly M. Hannum, Heather Champion, and Holly Downs

**Lead Contributors:** Tracy E. Patterson, Sarah Stawiski, Kelly M. Hannum, Heather Champion, Holly Downs

**Contributors:** Emily Hoole, Jennifer Martineau

**Director, People, Process, Products:** Davida Sharpe

**Manager, Publication Development:** Peter Scisco

**Editor:** Stephen Rush

**Associate Editor:** Shaun Martin

**Design and Illustrations:** Joanne Ferguson

**Rights and Permissions:** Kelly Lombardino



**Library of Congress Cataloging-in-Publication Data**

Names: Hannum, Kelly, author. | Patterson, Tracy E., 1956- author. | Stawiski, Sarah, 1976- author.
Title: Evaluating the impact of leadership development / Tracy E. Patterson, Sarah Stawiski, Kelly M. Hannum, Heather Champion, Holly Downs.
Description: 2nd edition. | Greensboro, NC : Center for Creative Leadership, [2017] | Includes bibliographical references and index.
Identifiers: LCCN 2017003189 (print) | LCCN 2017016242 (ebook) | ISBN 9781604916478 | ISBN 9781604916461 (alk. paper)
Subjects: LCSH: Leadership--Evaluation. | Executives--Training of--Evaluation.
Classification: LCC HD57.7 (ebook) | LCC HD57.7 .M39257 2017 (print) | DDC 658.4/092--dc23
LC record available at https://lccn.loc.gov/2017003189

CCL No. 001006
978-1-60491-646-1 – Print
978-1-60491-647-8 – Ebook

# CONTENTS

# PREFACE

In 2008 the Center for Creative Leadership (CCL), through its partner Pfeiffer (at that time an imprint of John Wiley & Sons but since rebranded), published *Evaluating the Impact of Leadership Development*, by Kelly M. Hannum and Jennifer W. Martineau. Building on the work of Hannum and Martineau, CCL has continued to grow and develop its practice of evaluating its programs, products, and services—efforts it started in the early 1970s. This revised edition of *Evaluating the Impact of Leadership Development* reflects the work of the broader group of CCL evaluators who continue these efforts today in collaboration with colleagues, collaborators, and clients. For decades CCL has designed and conducted evaluations for clients in the corporate, government, nonprofit, and educational sectors on six continents, giving us a global as well as contextual perspective.

Our goal with this revised edition is to continue CCL's tradition of sharing what we learn from our work with a broad range of professionals who practice in the fields of leadership development and its evaluation. Our aim is to add to the available information about the processes and tools used in evaluating leadership development. This book is a practical guide for human-resource professionals, consultants, managers, employees, and volunteers who have leadership-development responsibilities and want to enhance their knowledge and skills in fulfilling those responsibilities and to demonstrate the value of their work.

As with the previous edition, we have combined basic education about evaluation with examples of evaluation design processes and tools specific to leadership development. This information gives individuals with or without evaluation training—but who have some behavioral-sciences knowledge or experience in the organizational-development field—an understanding of what it takes to design, implement, report on, and use evaluation findings about the impact of leadership development on individuals, groups, organizations, and communities. Although reading this book will not make you an expert evaluator, we have presented a broad array of tools and processes from which readers can choose when designing and conducting their own evaluations.

For this edition we have updated, edited, and added to the solid foundation of the 2008 edition. We have organized the present edition according to the stages of the evaluation cycle introduced in Chapter One. Next, in Chapter Two, we outline the steps in the first phase of the cycle: gathering information and planning and conceptualizing the evaluation. In this chapter we have updated our guidance on identifying stakeholders, surfacing expectations, defining outcomes, and understanding the initiative design. We added sections on evaluating virtual initiatives, creating a results framework, and developing rubrics.

In Chapter Three we added a table that shows the advantages and disadvantages of the most commonly used data-collection methods and updated the sample forms and advice based on our more recent experience and perspectives. We have updated references to resources that we think are helpful for developing a deeper understanding or skill set that we were not able to fully address in this book or that may not be relevant for everyone. In Chapter Four we focus on interpreting and communicating results, the third phase of the evaluation cycle. In this chapter we added tips on data visualization and using rubrics to engage stakeholders in interpreting results. Chapter Five, a new chapter, outlines the final phase of the cycle: implementing changes and sharing lessons learned. In Chapter Six, also a chapter that was added in this edition, we focus on the future with emerging issues, trends, and future directions in leadership development and evaluation that we think are worthy of attention.

Given the fact that we have based this book on our experiences and collaborative work, there are more people who have contributed to this work than we could possibly name. We are especially grateful to our reviewers and CCL's editorial staff. We extend our thanks to Jennifer Martineau, Emily Hoole, Steve Rush, Pete Scisco, and Judy Turpin. We also want to thank our CCL research and evaluation colleagues: Anand Chandrasekar, Kristin Cullen-Lester, Regina Eckert, Valerie Ehrlich, Mike Raper, Micela Leis, and Stephen Young. Some of the examples used in the book are related to their work. We would like to acknowledge our CCL colleagues and clients who have collaborated and learned with us in the pursuit of a deeper understanding of the impact of leadership development. We also thank those acknowledged in the previous edition of this book. Finally, and most important, we are grateful to our friends and family, who provide us with ongoing support, encouragement, and understanding.

# FOREWORD

*Results that matter.* That phrase is significant for CCL. We specialize in leadership development—*only* leadership development—and do so to help individuals, teams, organizations, and communities achieve the results that matter to them. It is our mission to advance the understanding, practice, and development of leadership for the benefit of society worldwide. Our mission and our commitment to results that matter demand that we proactively evaluate our leadership-development initiatives thoroughly so that we can understand what makes them most effective and gives them maximum impact for the long term. This approach to evaluation requires complex, multifaceted, longitudinal designs and methods that are culturally and contextually appropriate for the audiences we serve. It demands that we not only use the best of what is available in the field of evaluation but also create new approaches and methods to meet our specific needs. And because our mission challenges us to share what we learn with the broader fields of leadership development and evaluation, we are delighted to offer you this book on evaluation.

Once upon a time (not too many years ago—as recently as the 1990s), the resources available for professionals engaged in the evaluation of leadership-development activities were few and far between. There were case studies published that provided examples of evaluations that had been conducted, but few of these studies included the evaluation methods used to collect, analyze, and interpret data. Books and other resources on general evaluation were available and could be used as a starting point, but they often required significant modification (and therefore expertise) to customize them for leadership development. Consultants were available but prohibitively expensive for many organizations to employ.

During this time CCL had been conducting evaluation studies with its clients and—at the request of these clients—began offering evaluation workshops for members of their staffs so that the clients could take on some evaluation activities themselves. Helping our clients was more than altruistic—it was in our best interest for clients to evaluate our leadership-development activities (and those of other providers) using the rigor and relevance of methods, processes, and approaches that we would use ourselves.

We started our workshops by instilling what we called an *evaluation mindset*—an array of beliefs that supported our clients in approaching evaluation from a collaborative, learning, and outcome- and process-oriented perspective. We then introduced our clients to a wide variety of evaluation methodologies and approaches to give them maximum flexibility to meet the nature of their leadership-development initiatives' design, audience, stakeholder group, and intended outcomes. We provided opportunities to apply evaluation to their leadership-development initiatives, with guidance from our evaluators.

The evaluation workshops were well-received and popular, yet they left our clients without two key resources for their ongoing use—continued guidance from CCL evaluators and a toolkit of the methods and processes we had introduced. To address the latter, the concept for the evaluation fieldbook was born.

The first edition of our evaluation book, *Evaluating the Impact of Leadership Development* (Hannum & Martineau, 2008), was intended as a rich resource for professionals responsible for evaluating leadership-development activities. Those with evaluation training or experience benefited from the specific focus on leadership development. Those without such training benefited from the methodologies, processes, and approaches useful in evaluation generally, and especially the evaluation of leadership development.

With this second edition, my colleagues at CCL have advanced the content and contribution significantly—I believe you will discover they have done a marvelous job. This book contains a wealth of experience, approach and philosophy, methodology, process, and general guidance.

In the years since publication of the first edition, CCL's evaluation practice has expanded along with that of the field at large. As leadership-development approaches entered the digital domain, so did our evaluation approaches. As CCL's leadership-development solutions expanded from a focus on individual, to team, to organization development, the evaluation practice was intentionally integrated as a means of continuous improvement and learning. The authors developed new approaches to provide evaluative insights and contributions to our clients and our leadership-solutions practitioners. And as CCL's leadership-development solutions have been made contextually relevant and available around the world for new leadership audiences including youths, rural village leaders, and self-organizing community groups, the authors have again prototyped new approaches to evaluation that are appropriate for the context. In this edition they share that knowledge and approach with you, their audience.

As you read this book, I encourage you to explore the knowledge and tools available to you in its pages. Once you have familiarized yourself with the full content, you will be able to use specific pages or specific sections that are most relevant to your leadership-development evaluation needs at the time.

I am proud of my colleagues for the exceptional work they do when evaluating leadership-development initiatives and I'm thrilled that they have shared so much of what their experience has taught them with other professionals doing similar work.

*Jennifer Martineau*
*Senior Vice President*
*Research, Evaluation, and Societal Advancement*
*Center for Creative Leadership*

# INTRODUCTION

A constant drive for effective stewardship of resources and for positive impact pushes commercial and not-for-profit organizations to weigh options and balance trade-offs for a wide array of endeavors, including investments in leadership development. Evaluation provides a logical and practical framework for collecting, assimilating, and communicating information related to decisions about what to include in a leadership-development initiative, how to best deliver the initiative, who should participate, how to get the most value out of the investment, and, finally, when to redirect resources. The approach to evaluation presented in this book can be applied in a variety of contexts, such as leadership-development programs for students or community leaders, but our focus is the evaluation of leadership-development initiatives in organizational settings.

Leadership and leadership development have transformed in recent decades and will continue to evolve as technological advances and social and political structures shift. The pace of change can make it feel as though one is trying to measure a moving target. Although much has changed and continues to change, we at CCL continue to see leadership broadly as the ability of people to achieve direction, alignment, and commitment together, and by extension we see leadership development as the means to create and enhance that capacity. Understanding how to do that appropriately and effectively, across a wide variety of settings, is the focus of our work as an organization, and evaluation plays a critical role.

Our expertise in leadership-development evaluation is coupled with a responsibility to share what we've learned. Our experience evaluating leadership-development initiatives across sectors and all over the world has given us specific insights for how that work should be conceived and conducted. We believe that evaluation should

- be collaborative;
- be integrated with discovery, design, and implementation;
- focus on the objectives and outcomes of the initiative;
- create a picture of overall impact; and
- facilitate learning.

Using a collaborative approach means involving key stakeholders—people who are or will be affected by the initiative being evaluated or by the outcomes of the evaluation itself. If lessons from an evaluation are to be successfully applied, relevant stakeholders must be involved in the planning or, at minimum, be informed about the initiative and the evaluation. As much as possible, they should also be involved in the interpretation of results and the creation of action plans based on the results; this ensures that the evaluation takes into account their perspectives and will secure their endorsement of the results and the plans that arise from them. A collaborative approach also provides a more balanced and comprehensive perspective on overall impact.

Ideally, the design of an evaluation is tightly integrated with the design of the initiative it evaluates. Both activities require a clear understanding of the intended objectives and outcomes of the initiative and engagement across stakeholder groups. When collaborative processes are used early on to focus the initiative and the evaluation simultaneously, the purposes, processes, roles, and responsibilities associated with both efforts are aligned and clarified.

Evaluation helps a variety of people and groups make informed decisions about how to improve leadership-development initiatives and examine the degree to which development goals have been accomplished. If outcomes aren't met, evaluation provides evidence about why outcomes were not met, thereby enabling people to learn from the experience and apply those lessons to improve effectiveness. These characteristics make evaluation not only important but also necessary for success.

## Evaluation-Design Guidelines

Following the evaluation-design guidelines described below will help you improve the quality of the evidence you collect and present—making it more difficult for others to dismiss evaluation findings as an anomaly or the result of some measurement fluke or design flaw. Following these guidelines does not guarantee defensible results but it does improve the likelihood that you can gather and present powerful evidence of impact. We offer these guidelines as the essential elements of good evaluation. Additional guidance on evaluation practice is provided by the Joint Committee on Standards for Educational Evaluation (www.jcsee.org).

**WHO? Examine impact from multiple perspectives.** Different stakeholder groups may have different perspectives on the impact of an initiative. Although one perspective might be considered more relevant than others, evaluators should consider all relevant perspectives. Participants, initiative staff, organizational leaders, and others may directly observe or experience the type of changes you want to assess. So it is most effective to collect relevant data from those individuals to create a full and accurate picture of impact.

**WHAT? Assess the different types and levels of change that can be observed.** Developing leadership capacity often involves multiple types of change (for example, new knowledge that brings enhanced self-awareness and prompts skill development). Changes in individuals often include knowledge and awareness gains and behavioral change in specific areas addressed in the initiative. Those funding the initiative often expect that the development of significant numbers of individuals will lead to improvements beyond the individual, such as improvements in organization-level indicators. Although changes in individuals may foster organizational results, this isn't guaranteed. The connections between the different levels of change need to be made as explicit as possible. If you measure changes along the way and analyze the connections between them, you are more likely to understand why a development initiative did or did not have the desired impact.

**WHEN? Look at change over time.** Leadership-development efforts often have short-term, midrange, and long-term results. Limiting your evaluation to participants' reactions immediately after an event, or even 30 days following the event, may seem like an efficient way to quickly wrap up a study, but accomplishing significant change can take longer than that. There may be a period of reduced performance while participants are learning and practicing new skills, which is not necessarily an indication that a development initiative has failed. If your evaluation looks only at the short-term results, it may not reveal significant long-term impact or may miss the opportunity to learn how to enhance long-term and more significant impact. Design your plan to measure change at multiple, and appropriate, points in time. One way of determining the effect of a development initiative is to gather data from those in the participant group before they participate in the initiative. Then you can look at trends of growth related to the period of time before the initiative and compare them with trends that occur during and after.

**HOW? Use multiple data-collection methods.** Each data-collection method is suited for different purposes and has its own benefits and shortcomings. An evaluation design that uses multiple methods can reveal information about different kinds of impact that stakeholders expect and can provide you with a comprehensive picture of change. For example, behavioral change might be best captured by a 360-degree instrument designed to measure change, but face-to-face interviews may be the best way to understand the obstacles people face in implementing desired behavioral changes. End-of-initiative evaluation surveys might be the best way to measure participants' immediate response to a training initiative, but they don't reveal the results of individual development in the way that post-initiative questionnaires and interviews can. Although not feasible in all circumstances, an approach that thoughtfully combines qualitative and quantitative data—called a *mixed-methods approach*—can be an elegant way to design a comprehensive evaluation.

**SO WHAT? Use evidence to make evaluative judgments.** One of the hallmarks of a good evaluation is that it provides stakeholders with a sense of how well something is working. To do that effectively, you have to know how success is defined and measured by different stakeholder groups. In some cases there is an established and agreed-upon benchmark (which could be something as simple as showing that participants are significantly better at something than they were before the initiative); in other cases you might need to work with stakeholders to define what success would look like and what data are appropriate to consider. This kind of interpretation and sensemaking is often best accomplished by or with the facilitation of an evaluator. Descriptive data about what happened during and after an initiative is important, but the true value of evaluation is making meaning from those data in order to learn from and use the information to make informed choices.

In the previous edition of this book, using control groups was listed as a design guideline. Using control groups for comparison helps you answer questions about (1) whether changes found in your evaluation are the result of the leadership-development intervention and not of some other factor and (2) whether this particular initiative is better than alternatives. However, identifying and gaining access to a group of people with characteristics (age, job type, and prior training, for example) that are similar to those of the people participating in the development initiative and in a similar context can be nearly impossible in some situations. In our experience we have rarely been able to use a control-group design (which is why we have downgraded it from a guideline to something to consider when feasible and appropriate). It can work when (1) a control group is a viable and ethical option, (2) the intervention is the only known systematic difference between the groups, and (3) nothing unusual occurred during the intervention and evaluation periods. However, there are often significant barriers to using this approach and it does not always yield the most accurate or valuable data. More information about using control groups in leadership-development evaluations can be found in Chapter One of *The Handbook of Leadership Development Evaluation* (Hannum, Martineau, & Reinelt, 2007).

Now that you have a sense of our purpose for writing this book and our overall approach to evaluation, it is time to look more closely at what evaluation is and how to use it in organizations.

# 1 CHAPTER ONE
# Understanding the Evaluation Function and Process

Because you are reading this book, you have probably already decided you are interested in evaluating leadership development, but you may not be clear about the purpose of the evaluation or how you want to go about evaluating an initiative. There are many reasons to evaluate leadership development and many ways to go about it. A significant portion of this book is designed to help uncover the purposes specific to your situation; this is because understanding the underlying purpose of an evaluation is the first step in designing an effective evaluation.

## Evaluation Approaches and Purposes

Evaluation approaches are often categorized as developmental, formative, or summative.

Developmental evaluation is typically used in adaptive and emergent situations to bring an ongoing evaluation perspective and process to inform the initiative as it unfolds so it can respond to a changing environment or better reflect a new understanding of the context and the needs. In a developmental approach, the function of the evaluator is mainly to work with stakeholders over time to define success, gather and interpret information that helps shape the emergent design and implementation, and help stakeholders identify what new courses of action are needed throughout a process of development.

Formative evaluation also informs the design and delivery of an initiative but is used when the process and situation are more fixed and defined. The purpose of formative evaluation is to gather information that can be used to improve and enhance an intervention.

Summative evaluation is more focused on the end of an intervention, when its value or benefit can be determined to inform future decision making.

An evaluation of an initiative may include phases that range in approach from developmental (in the early phase) to summative (in the latter phase). Listed below are some of the common purposes of evaluation; the type of approach these tend to be associated with is included in parentheses.

- To understand leadership-development needs (developmental, formative)
- To improve leadership-development efforts by surfacing expectations, articulating outcomes, and challenging assumptions (developmental, formative)
- To assess the impact of leadership-development efforts (summative)
- To provide information that will help in making decisions about investing in leadership development (summative)

Although it is important to understand the purposes of evaluation, it is also helpful to consider the dangers of not evaluating. For example, if you don't evaluate you will not

- know if an initiative achieved what was intended;
- be able to inform stakeholders, who won't have evaluation results to use in planning;
- learn lessons that could improve initiative design and implementation; or
- have information that can support continued or future funding.

## Types of Evaluators

Evaluators come from a variety of educational and professional backgrounds. Research and evaluation are often seen as involving the same tasks and skill sets. However, although the two can be very similar, there are important distinctions. Evaluation traditionally focuses on determining the quality, effectiveness, or value of something, while research seeks to understand relationships among variables or describe phenomena in order to develop knowledge that can be generalized. When possible, it is good to seek people who have extensive evaluation experience and training that is relevant to the context in which the leadership-development initiative is operating.

In general, evaluators can be classified as internal evaluators or external evaluators. Internal evaluators are part of the initiative, organization, or community in which they conduct evaluations and are employed by the group that provides the leadership development. External evaluators are contracted from outside the initiative, organization, or community in which leadership development is taking place. Internal evaluators usually have the benefit of a deep understanding of the context of the initiative and evaluation. They may also have existing credibility and trusting relationships that enable them to gather data that are more relevant and candid than data gathered by an outsider. However, because they are part of the organization or group they are evaluating, internal evaluators may be seen as biased and may also take aspects of the context or initiative for granted, whereas external evaluators would probe more deeply and challenge assumptions. External evaluators have the benefit of being able to ask questions that might seem naive or disruptive if asked by internal evaluators. External evaluators may also seem more objective to stakeholders. If an evaluation requires asking sensitive questions, an external evaluator may be a better choice because individuals may be more willing to share that information confidentially with someone from the outside. However, external evaluators may not fully understand the context of the initiative and evaluation, and may therefore be less sensitive to potentially offensive language or more likely to make recommendations or choose approaches that are less relevant.

If at all possible, a combination of internal and external evaluators brings the best of both roles to the evaluation; their strengths complement each other. If funding is not sufficient for both and only internal evaluators are used, another strategy is to use an external evaluator as an adviser for certain parts of the evaluation. Doing so will cost less than using an external evaluator to conduct the evaluation and will provide some of the credibility and fresh insight associated with external perspectives. This is not to suggest that internal evaluators lack credibility but rather that some organizations place value on external perspectives that should be considered.

If you are pursuing an internal-evaluation approach but do not have individuals trained in evaluation, consider investing in training for those selected or volunteering to conduct evaluation. There are many colleges and universities that offer face-to-face as well as online courses in evaluation, as well as evaluation groups that offer workshops. If money is not available for courses or workshops, you may want to build a small library, or at least purchase a book, to help build evaluation capacity. The book you are holding is a great start to building a library. Additionally, Hallie Preskill and Darlene Russ-Eft's book *Building Evaluation Capacity: 72 Activities for Teaching and Training* (2015) is a practical choice. E. Jane Davidson's *Evaluation Methodology Basics: The Nuts and Bolts of Sound Evaluation* (2005) is also a helpful guide.

Another way to build capacity is to start an evaluation learning group. The group could meet to discuss shared reading on evaluation and to help think through evaluation issues. Some evaluation consultants offer evaluation-coaching services. Evaluation coaching usually entails a professional evaluator working with an individual or group to ask questions and provide advice and resources that enable the individual or group to conduct evaluation but with expert support. This approach can be helpful for organizations that have a very new evaluation function and wish to develop greater capacity for conducting internal evaluations.

## Evaluator Roles

Once you have identified an evaluator or group of evaluators, take time to clarify role expectations. Evaluators can play many roles, so it can be risky to assume that everyone has the same expectations. The list below (adapted from Hannum, Martineau, & Reinelt, 2007, pp. 8–9) outlines the common roles played by evaluators. These are not mutually exclusive; an evaluator can play a combination of roles as well as different roles over the course of an evaluation.

- *Assessor.* Evaluators assess the value and quality of a leadership-development initiative or intervention to determine if it has achieved its desired outcomes or provided a valuable return on investment.
- *Planner and designer.* Evaluators assist stakeholders in using evaluation findings and processes to improve an existing initiative or design a new one. They also engage designers to identify which outcomes are desired, what success will look like, and what program elements will contribute to or cause these outcomes.
- *Trainer and capacity builder.* Evaluators educate stakeholders so they can design, implement, and use evaluation effectively. Often this is done by facilitating gatherings at which stakeholders participate in the evaluation process and learn how to use evaluation tools.
- *Translator and boundary spanner.* Evaluators cross boundaries to listen to and search for multiple perspectives and interpretations. As they move back and forth across boundaries, evaluators carry perspectives and findings with them and

share these with the other groups in ways that those groups can hear and understand.

- *Coach, critical friend, and partner.* Evaluators can coach individuals to reflect on the data and their own knowledge of the process and overall project to help direct strategy toward bettering the process and ultimately the overall initiative. This coaching role embraces and supports the developmental changes that occur throughout the initiative and evaluation life cycle and supports practitioners in being thoughtful and reflective in their approach.

- *Advocate.* Evaluators present evaluation findings in public forums that are intended to influence decisions about an initiative, policy direction, or allocation of resources. Evaluators can give voice to ideas, perspectives, and knowledge that normally go unheard or unknown because the groups that espouse them are ignored by groups with more resources and power. Evaluators advocate for taking the time and investing the resources to reflect, inquire, study, and assess initiatives because this process increases the likelihood of success and impact. In their role as advocate, evaluators may find that they are asked to modify or couch their findings in ways that will have positive results for a particular audience. Evaluators have an ethical obligation to do their best to maintain the integrity of the evaluation.

- *Reflective practitioner.* Evaluators learn from their own thoughts, reactions, and experiences through a systematic process of interaction, inquiry, and reflection (see Chapters Four and Seven in Hannum, Martineau, & Reinelt, 2007).

## The Context for Evaluation

Because people have different worldviews and value systems, proper data gathering, synthesis, and interpretation requires more than blindly applying a set of tools. To be relevant and valid, data collection, analysis, and dissemination strategies need to "take into account potential cultural and linguistic barriers; include a reexamination of established evaluation measures for cultural appropriateness; and/or incorporate creative strategies for ensuring culturally competent analysis and creative dissemination of findings to diverse audiences" (Inouye, Cao Yu, & Adefuin, 2005, p. 6). Understanding the cultural context and practicing culturally competent evaluation involve an appreciation of how history, culture, and place shape ways of knowing and the ways in which knowledge is used. If you are working in a culturally diverse context (and almost every context is), take the time to examine and understand how cultural differences may influence or impact leadership development and its evaluation.

Leadership-development initiatives do not have to occur in different countries for culture to matter to your evaluation. Chances are that there are cultural differences within an organization that affect how evaluation should be designed and implemented. Cultural differences can exist between countries, regions, organizations, industries, professions, and other groups of people. For instance, in some departments there may be a culture of giving direct feedback and having honest dialogue about an experience, whereas in other departments people may be more guarded about providing feedback. While a focus group or group debrief may work well in the first context, methods that protect confidentiality (for example, individual reflection and surveys) may work better in the second. As noted in the American Evaluation Association's Statement on Cultural Competence in Evaluation (http://www.eval.org/p/cm/ld/fid=92), cultural competence is important because it is respectful of stakeholders and supports the validity of the evaluation, implying that there is a greater likelihood of drawing accurate and useful conclusions.

People can have very different ideas about and experiences with leadership development and evaluation. Asking questions of different stakeholder groups and reviewing existing information about the initiative and the organization can offer insight into the beliefs and practices of those stakeholders with respect to leadership development and evaluation.

## Evaluation as a Process

This book provides an overview of the essential phases of the evaluation process, as depicted in Figure 1.1. The first phase, *Gather Information, Plan, and Conceptualize* the evaluation, is described in Chapter Two. This phase includes learning and planning activities that guide evaluators and others toward results that are relevant and beneficial. Activities that focus an evaluation include the following:

- identifying stakeholders and their expectations for the initiative and for the evaluation;
- connecting with the initiative design;
- determining the purpose of the initiative and the evaluation;
- confirming the resources available;

- determining the level and type of impact;
- surfacing expectations; and
- drafting evaluation questions and potential data-collection methods.

Figure 1.1 – Evaluation as a Process

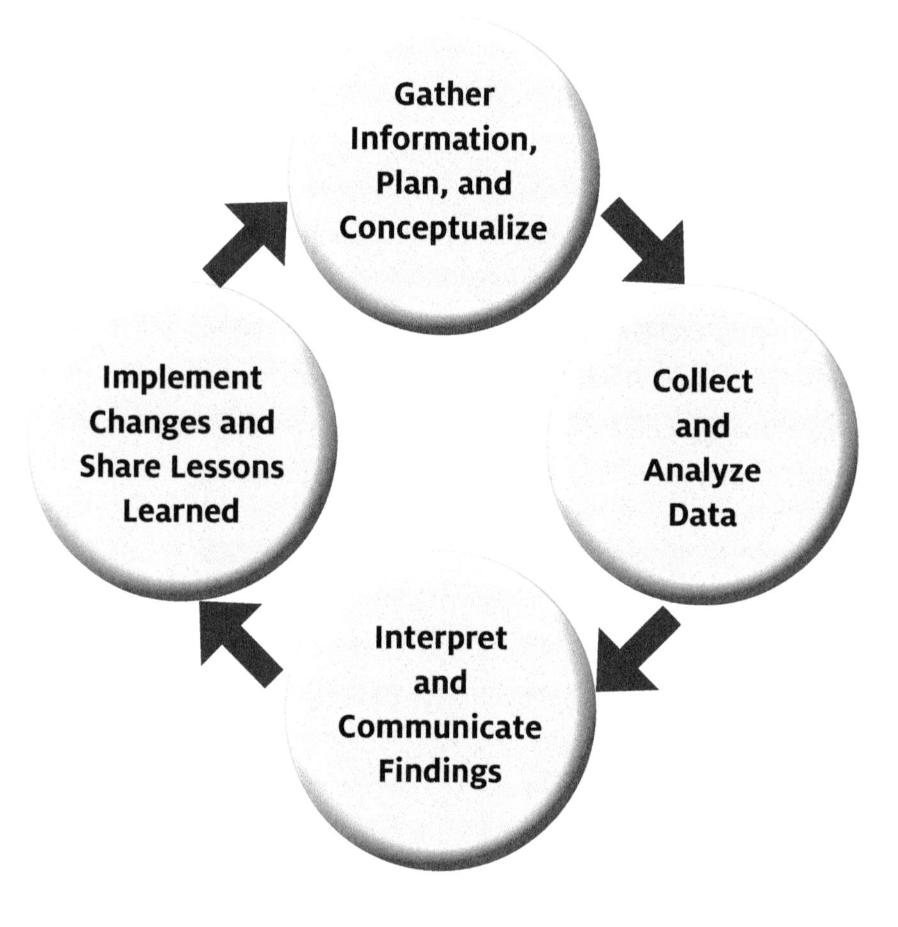

Ideally, evaluators conduct these activities in conjunction with the design or implementation of the initiative. The complexity of contexts and cultures combined with the complexity of developing leaders requires these processes to help stakeholders develop a common understanding of issues, purposes, and roles. Combining the design phases of the evaluation and the initiative helps ensure the utility and efficiency of both processes. As you focus your evaluation, this combination will help you ask the appropriate people the right questions. At the end of this phase you will have developed your evaluation plan.

Chapter Three provides information needed for the next phase of the evaluation process: collecting and analyzing data. In this phase, evaluators and key stakeholders implement the evaluation plan. Measuring and interpreting change resulting from leadership development is a complex endeavor. It's in this phase that you will address research-design considerations such as using multiple data-collection techniques. The information stakeholders provided during the focusing phase can be used to explore the benefits, drawbacks, and caveats associated with different evaluation techniques so you can find the right fit.

In Chapter Four we provide guidance for the phase of interpreting and communicating findings from the evaluation. Since the first edition of this book we have seen significant advances in strategies and techniques for making data easy to interpret and for being more inclusive and transparent when sharing information.

In Chapter Five we address the essential steps in the final phase in the cycle: implementing changes based on evaluation findings and reflecting on lessons learned. This phase is often overlooked. Typically, the results of the evaluation are compiled and reported by the evaluation team, which includes evaluators and perhaps some key stakeholders (for example, program staff, program sponsor, and selected participants). This team may make preliminary recommendations for action, but the conversation often ends there. Our position is that learning and action are the ultimate goals of a well-conceived and professionally produced evaluation. Delivering a report with recommendations isn't enough to realize that goal. Implementing and monitoring the action plan that arises from your evaluation helps ensure that such learning will take place.

In Chapter Six, the final chapter, we briefly discuss emerging issues, trends, and future directions that have direct implications on how evaluations of leadership development are designed and implemented. As mentioned in the introduction, evaluation and leadership-development theories and practice are evolving quickly. As professionals who span both fields, we offer our perspective on the opportunities and challenges ahead.

# CHAPTER TWO
## Gather Information, Plan, and Conceptualize the Evaluation

This chapter focuses on developing a deep understanding of the initiative's purpose and design as well as the perspectives of key stakeholders. The ideal time to plan an evaluation is when the development initiative is being designed. Asking evaluation questions can help stakeholders understand the desired impact of the development initiative in concrete terms. That information can be used to design the initiative in a way that will likely promote the desired results. However, it is not always possible to plan an evaluation during the design of the initiative. Often those funding or conducting leadership development don't realize the need for an evaluation until after the initiative has been conducted. Even if you are in that situation, it's not too late for an evaluation. Although far from ideal, some evaluation is better than none. Evaluations can be conducted retrospectively, and the ideas shared in this chapter can be applied in those situations as well.

Whether the evaluation is designed in unison with the creation of the development initiative or designed after participants complete the process, it's essential to define the key elements of the evaluation design. The following actions can help you successfully gather the information you will need to design an effective evaluation.

- *Identify and engage stakeholders.* Who will be affected by the development initiative and its evaluation? Who is most interested in the evaluation findings?
- *Surface expectations and define the purpose of the initiative.* What are the reasons behind the development initiative? What results do stakeholders expect? When do they expect those results?
- *Understand the initiative design.* Who is the target audience? What will its experience entail? How is the initiative being delivered (face-to-face, blended, virtual, asynchronous, or synchronous)? What are the expected outcomes of the initiative?
- *Create a results framework.* Is the initiative designed in a way that is likely to achieve the desired results? If not, what aspects of the design should be modified?
- *Determine the evaluation questions.* How can stakeholder expectations be reflected in the evaluation questions?
- *Create an evaluation plan.* How will the evaluation gather data, from whom, and when? What resources will be used? How will results be communicated to stakeholders and when?

## Identify and Engage Stakeholders

Stakeholders are people who are, or will be, affected by the initiative being evaluated or by the outcomes of the evaluation itself. If they do not get their questions answered or do not feel their perspective is represented, it's unlikely that your evaluation will serve its purpose, no matter how rigorous your design. To avoid this disappointment and to get the highest-quality, most-relevant data possible, identify and include stakeholders early in the evaluation-design process and understand the different perspectives and power dynamics at play. To identify the key stakeholders, ask the following questions:

- Who has an interest in the development initiative?
- Who has an interest in the evaluation's process and results?
- Are there additional people whose support is required for the success of the initiative or the evaluation?
- Who has decision-making authority with respect to both the initiative and the evaluation?

Once the key stakeholders have been identified, clarify their interests and expectations about why and how the evaluation is being conducted so that any differences in expectations can be addressed. Later we will examine stakeholder perspectives on the initiative itself, but for now the focus is on the evaluation.

## Table 2.1 – Stakeholder Evaluation Interests

| Stakeholder Group | What Will They Want to Know from the Evaluation? | When and How Can Evaluation Information Best Be Shared? |
|---|---|---|
| Initiative Staff | What worked well? What could have been better? Were participants adequately supported in their development?<br><br>What were the benefits of conducting the initiative?<br><br>Did stakeholders think the initiative "worked"?<br><br>What's next for the initiative? | Communicate throughout the initiative so adjustments can be made along the way.<br><br>Share and discuss findings at the end of the initiative. |
| Initiative Participants | What were the benefits of the initiative?<br><br>How did the individual participant's experience compare with that of others in the initiative? | Make sure intended benefits were explained before the initiative.<br><br>Provide data throughout the experience (if appropriate).<br><br>Share final evaluation findings. |
| Senior Organizational Leaders | What were the organizational benefits of the initiative?<br><br>What were the expectations and requirements of providing the initiative?<br><br>How can we get the most value out of the initiative moving forward?<br><br>Was the initiative worth it? | Confirm shared understanding of intended benefits and expectations early in the process (via a short discussion or presentation).<br><br>Share a summary of the final evaluation findings and implications. |

## Table 2.1 – Stakeholder Evaluation Interests (continued)

| Stakeholder Group | What Will They Want to Know from the Evaluation? | When and How Can Evaluation Information Best Be Shared? |
|---|---|---|
| Managers (with Direct Reports) Participating in the Initiative | How did this initiative benefit my group?<br><br>What were the benefits of the initiative?<br><br>What contributed to those benefits? | Confirm shared understanding of the intended benefits and expectations early in the process (via a short discussion or presentation).<br><br>Share a summary of the final evaluation findings and implications. |
| Managers (without Direct Reports) Participating in the Initiative | What were the benefits of the initiative?<br><br>How might these help my group in the future?<br><br>How would someone in my group access the initiative? (Will there be another one, and if so, when?)<br><br>What was learned from the evaluation that would be helpful? | Final report (perhaps as an infographic).<br><br>Summary of evaluation highlights in organizational newsletters or memos. |

Identifying stakeholders and understanding their perspectives must be part of an ongoing process. Although it is critical to do so early in evaluation planning, reexamining who key stakeholders are and what they are interested in or expect is good practice, particularly if it is a complex, multiyear evaluation. Engaging stakeholders throughout the evaluation will likely result in an evaluation that is more relevant and useful.

## Surface Expectations and Define the Purpose of the Initiative

The purpose of a development initiative may seem to be clear, but often, when you check your understanding against that of different stakeholder groups, you will find a lack of alignment. Working with stakeholders to surface their expectations for the initiative and helping them reach a shared understanding of its purpose helps bring clarity to the type of evaluation that will be most useful. Designing a development initiative and its evaluation at the same time is an effective way to ensure that stakeholders have that alignment and understanding. Defining how your evaluation will measure the impact of the development initiative puts abstract goals (such as "We will develop better leaders") into practical terms (such as "Our senior managers will understand how to give feedback to their direct reports").

Understanding stakeholder assumptions will help you better define the purpose of the initiative so you can design a more effective evaluation. Although not all stakeholders will, or should, participate in determining the scope or focus of the evaluation, it will be helpful to you to understand all of the assumptions the stakeholder groups hold about the purposes of the development initiative. A thorough understanding of how elements of the development initiative fit together and the context in which the initiative takes place are needed to design the evaluation. Integrating the design of the evaluation with the design of the initiative prompts clear conversations about stakeholder expectations at a time when adjustments can be made to make sure that both the initiative and the evaluation are on track to deliver on those expectations. With guidance, stakeholders should be able to articulate the type and amount of impact they expect, as well as the expected timing of that impact.

In reviewing the leadership-development initiative, evaluators can gain a full picture of the process by discussing expectations with stakeholders. The following list of questions can be helpful in guiding these discussions with key stakeholders.

**Exhibit 2.1 – Questions for Surfacing Expectations and Defining Purpose**

*Overall Purpose (or Development Strategy)*

- What specific challenge does the initiative hope to address?
- How does the initiative support the organization's business or leadership strategy?
- What specific leadership needs does the initiative address?
- Are there any other external and internal pressures or demands for creating the initiative?
- What is the overall purpose of the initiative?

*Expected Impact*

- What type of outcomes is the initiative intended to promote? Knowledge acquisition? Awareness change? Behavioral change? Skill development? Performance improvement? Network enhancement? Culture change?
- What type of impact is the initiative expected to have? Will it affect only individuals, or will it also affect teams or groups? Will it have a broad organizational impact?
- What conditions are needed for the initiative to be successful?
- When is it realistic to expect to see results? How will we know when these results have occurred?

## Defining and Categorizing Impact

The Kirkpatrick Four Levels is a widely used model for training evaluation (Kirkpatrick & Kirkpatrick, 2014). For many years the model has provided a common language for understanding among stakeholders about the kinds of outcomes that are expected from a training initiative, including leadership-development training. An increasing number of models are being used to evaluate training and development initiatives, such as the one offered by Bersin (2006), but Kirkpatrick remains prominent. We have found that stakeholders often expect us to frame our approach to an evaluation in terms of the levels in the Kirkpatrick model. As a reminder (or perhaps as a brief introduction), the model organizes the types of outcomes from training and development initiatives into four levels: Level 1 (Reactions, which includes Satisfaction, Engagement, and Relevance); Level 2 (Learning, which includes Knowledge, Skill, Attitude, Confidence, and Commitment); Level 3 (Behaviors, which includes Performance as well as the Processes and Systems that reinforce, encourage, and reward performance); and Level 4 (Results, including leading indicators). Commonly, measuring Level 1 is expected and routine, while measuring Levels 2, 3, and 4 is considered more challenging.

Although widely used and simple to understand, the Kirkpatrick model may not fully meet your needs for designing an evaluation of a leadership-development initiative because (1) not all leadership-development initiatives are limited to training (for example, they can include components such as consulting with executive teams, developing networks, and engaging in action-learning projects) and (2) the model as it is commonly referenced does not take into account the more complex factors that contribute to the impact of leadership development, such as how participants are selected and prepared for the initiative, how closely the design is aligned with the organizational needs it is meant to address, and the supports and barriers to learning transfer. That said, the Kirkpatrick model can be helpful when thinking about the depth of impact. It focuses on individual and organizational change, but change can be expected at other levels as well. Understanding where and what kinds of change are expected and linking that back to the initiative helps create a deeper understanding of impact and provides a framework for thinking about areas of potential disconnection between what is expected and what the initiative is designed to create.

Over the next few sections we'll briefly discuss various ways that leadership development can lead to impact at the individual, group, organizational, and societal levels. Every leadership-development initiative is intended to have some sort of an impact on the individuals who experience it, but some may also be designed to have an impact at collective levels.

Individuals. Although an impact on individuals is expected in leadership-development work, what that impact is can vary. For example, individuals may learn new leadership models and practices, or they may learn how to be effective with different types of people or in different contexts. Participants may develop an increased awareness of their personal leadership style and how it affects others. They might also change work-related behaviors or increase their effectiveness at using newly acquired skills. Impact can vary depending on the content and design of the initiative and the development needs of individual participants. For example, three- to five-day assessment-for-development initiatives are likely to result in participants acquiring critical knowledge, building awareness, and gaining ability to apply lessons to certain behaviors and situations. For changes to become ingrained in an individual's performance, additional developmental experiences, such as one-on-one coaching and challenging assignments, are necessary.

Groups. Development initiatives created for individual leaders can also have an impact at the group level. For example, a leader's group might perform more effectively after the leader has enhanced his or her leadership capability. The group may be able to get products to market more quickly because its manager has improved his or her skill in focusing group effort. After participating in a development initiative and learning skills that encourage better communication among team members, a leader may be able to guide the team toward more effectively supporting community goals. When development initiatives are targeted at intact teams, outcomes are more pronounced and more quickly observable because the team as a whole is able to put the members' new awareness, knowledge, and skills into practice immediately.

Organizations. When organizations invest substantial resources in developing leadership capabilities, they look for results that will help them achieve strategic objectives, sustain their effectiveness, and maintain their competitive position. The quality of an organization's leadership is only one contributing factor to reaching these goals. Even so, a leadership-development initiative can, among other things, facilitate culture change, enhance the organizational climate, improve the company's bottom line, and build a stronger, more influential organizational profile. An organization may also use development initiatives to augment the internal branding of the company, as is the case when a company offers development opportunities in order to present itself as an appealing place to work. With regard to evaluation, stakeholders will want to gather information that provides evidence of the link between leadership development and measures of organizational success. Further, organizations may take on initiatives that are focused on achieving results for the organization as a whole, rather than primarily for individual leaders. For instance, an organization could be working on changing its leadership culture. (See the sidebar "Evaluating Organizational-Leadership Initiatives.")

Societal. Leadership-development initiatives can also aim to have an impact on societal or system-level change (Hannum, Martineau, & Reinelt, 2007). Because these types of outcomes typically take longer to occur, it may be difficult to see them in the time frame of most evaluations. For these types of evaluations, evaluators look for changes in social norms, social networks, policies, allocation of resources, and quality-of-life indicators. In a corporate setting, for example, an organization could be motivated to provide leadership development designed to move an entire industry toward improving working conditions and safety for all employees. In a community context, where building networks is a core focus of the leadership-development effort, evaluators may look for changes in the diversity and composition of networks, levels of trust and connectedness, and capacity for collective action (Hoppe & Reinelt, 2010).

## Evaluating Organizational-Leadership Initiatives

In contrast to leadership initiatives that focus on enhancing individual leadership skills, organizational-leadership solutions focus on enhancing leadership capabilities for an entire organization. There are many approaches to developing organizational leadership, and many of them are not programmatic. For instance, a leadership team may choose to define and implement a new leadership strategy for its organization. This may entail making changes to talent systems, promoting a more collaborative culture, or even restructuring the organization to better support the strategy. It could also involve coaching of an executive team, using employee forums to conduct culture-change work, or launching action-learning teams, among many other possibilities.

Organizational-leadership initiatives are often multifaceted and complex. It may be more difficult to articulate clear outcomes and define a clear path to achieving the outcomes than is the case with individual leadership development. However, assessing the effectiveness of organizational-leadership initiatives is still important, perhaps more so than with individual initiatives. Many of the steps and approaches that would be recommended when evaluating leadership-development initiatives for individuals would still be useful for evaluating organizational-leadership initiatives. For instance, engaging stakeholders in conversations early on about expectations and what success would look like can help everyone be aligned about the initiative and can inform what to measure to assess the initiative's progress and success.

Evaluation of complex and adaptive initiatives requires continuous data gathering and collective sensemaking. *Developmental Evaluation* (Patton, 2011; see also Gamble, 2008) is one approach that offers promise for evaluation of organizational-leadership initiatives. Unlike traditional evaluation approaches, a developmental approach is particularly suited to adaptive work in complex and dynamic situations. In these situations, systematically gathering and sharing information helps to frame concepts, surface issues, and track development. Doing so can close the gap between guessing and knowing what is happening from different perspectives.

## Impact Over Time

If the impact of an initiative is expected to occur over a period of time, you can design your measurements to account for short-term, midrange, and long-term impact. The short-term impact of a development initiative can include what participants think about the initiative and their experience with it immediately after completion. Short-term impact also includes the development of new ideas or new self-awareness based on what participants have recently learned from their developmental experience.

To measure midrange impact on individuals, we recommend that the evaluation should occur three to six months after the development initiative ends or after key components of the initiative are delivered or experienced. Measurements at this time usually relate to individual skill improvement, behavioral change, or team development. Assessing a development initiative's long-term impact often occurs nine months to a year or more after the initiative ends, especially if the expected outcomes include promotions and enhanced leadership roles for participants. Areas that benefit most from this type of evaluation include the attainment of complex skills and organizational-level change. Changes in organizations take longer to achieve. Assessing change over time allows you to see trends and to determine when change occurs and if change is enduring.

## Understand the Initiative Design

Once the overall purpose of the initiative is understood, how it fits into the broader strategy for the organization has been established, and outcomes have been defined, the next step is to understand the proposed design (although in practice these steps often occur simultaneously). This section outlines some of the key elements of the design that are important to understand.

**Target population and participant selection.** The outcomes of a leadership-development initiative depend heavily on the individuals participating. The skills and perspectives they bring to the initiative and the context in which they work affect what they are able to learn and the results they are able to achieve. Therefore, it's critical that you fully understand the target population for the development initiative you are evaluating, including how participants were selected. Understanding the needs, concerns, and expectations that participants bring to the development process can help you measure the results of that process. Related to this, understanding how the participants are selected and whether they will participate as one group or as multiple cohorts is also key to designing the evaluation. We make a distinction between the target population and the participants in the initiative because differences can be created in the selection process. For example, if the target population is all middle managers but only managers from a specific geographic region are selected, that can be a cue to ask questions to understand the selection process and whether it might be biased in a manner that could undercut the desired impact. It may make sense to focus on a certain region initially, but in that case it may also make sense to examine organizational impact for only that region as well.

Organizational context. Because the success of a development initiative is affected by its context, evaluators may need to become familiar with the profile of the group of managers to whom participants report and the types of colleagues with whom participants work. The support and involvement of others has an impact on participants' ability to effectively integrate what they've learned and apply the skills they've acquired. Understanding what, if any, role these stakeholders have had in the process can provide a missing link when it comes to understanding impact. For example, if an initiative is seeking organizational change through a leadership-development initiative for high-potential leaders, but managers of high-potentials are resistant to these types of changes, then understanding that dynamic is important to the evaluation. It's also important to understand any practices or policies that are relevant to the initiative.

Duration of the initiative. Initiatives can vary widely in their duration. Understanding the duration of the initiative can help you identify when to look for different types of impact and also help calibrate the depth of impact sought. As you examine the duration of the initiative relative to the desired impact, ask yourself whether the length of the initiative seems adequate for fostering the desired level and types of results. For example, a two-hour workshop on leading across cultures may raise awareness but it is unlikely to lead to significant behavior change.

**Delivery mode.** Development designs usually have a road map that demonstrates the major elements of the initiative, how they are to be delivered (for example, face-to-face, virtually, or a blend of both), and the timing within and between each. For instance, if it is a traditional face-to-face initiative, what are the major components and outcomes expected? If there is a virtual-learning component, how many modules will be covered and over what period of time? Will these be short engagements for accelerated development? Will these engagements build on one another so that they must be done in chronological order, or will the initiative have more distributed control, being self-paced and user-controlled?

## Evaluating Virtual Initiatives

The substantial growth of digital- or virtual-learning offerings—including online modules, mobile learning, Massive Open Online Courses (MOOCs), and other virtual-learning opportunities—by leadership-development providers points to the need for increased understanding of evaluation beyond a traditional face-to-face context. CCL has also been offering and evaluating initiatives within the virtual space. Every evaluation will have similarities and differences regardless of the mode of delivery, but you will probably want to pay attention to the following tips if the initiative is situated in a digital space (Mehta & Downs, 2016):

- Include data-collection measures that focus not only on the content and experience of participants but also on their previous experiences with and attitudes toward the training-delivery mode. If a participant had to learn the platform and content, the cognitive load will be higher, and this might negatively impact his or her experience.

- Check all evaluation elements for appropriateness in the nontraditional digital or virtual space. Some characteristics that make a traditional face-to-face initiative successful may not directly translate without adjustment in the digital space; the same is true for the evaluation instruments. For instance, a standard survey that asks about something that can only occur in the face-to-face space needs to be tweaked or removed.

- Collect other information that might not normally be necessary or available in the face-to-face space. For instance, participant rates of time spent in the management system for online learning might be useful in talking about how much time is spent in the virtual classroom.

- Think carefully about data-collection timing and triggers. Participants who have experienced a self-paced online program might not have completed the program at the same time or in the same way. For instance, if some participants take a class and provide feedback before a company restructures and others are still taking the class online when the restructure is announced, the participant experiences and scores might be different before and after the event.

- Make sure the initiative objectives are clear and measurable; this is especially true in the digital environment. There is research in higher education that suggests that some instructors in the face-to-face environment are sometimes able to overcome weaker content alignment in part because they are charismatic and also possibly because they are more able to set the tone and clarify expectations in the moment. The digital environment often does not present as many opportunities to clarify expectations between the instructor and the students, so clear, measurable objectives are especially vital.

Design content. The content of the design includes the topics the initiative focuses on. Is the initiative based on a specific framework or theory of leadership? What leadership competencies are addressed? What mindset shifts are fostered? Are collaborative approaches addressed? What types of modules will be completed? How does the design ensure learning transfer? For example, does it engage participants in applying what they learn in the initiative to leadership challenges relevant to their work? Does it include strategies for participants to receive ongoing support for applying new skills from coaching sessions or from their supervisors or colleagues?

Existing sources of data. Data are often collected during the initiative that may be useful in an evaluation. It is helpful to identify what data are already being gathered as part of the initiative or by other groups or departments that may be useful in an evaluation. The risk here is using what's available even though it may not be that useful in the evaluation. Do, however, think carefully about whether the data available are a good fit for the evaluation. If there's a match, then by all means use what's available. Conversely, when you design your data-collection efforts you may find ways to weave collection of evaluation data into the initiative experience. For example, having participants reflect on and document what they learned and how they have changed can be a source of evaluation data as well as part of the development experience.

The following questions can be used to gain an understanding of the initiative design and round out your overall picture of the initiative.

## Exhibit 2.2 – Understanding the Initiative Design

Use this worksheet to get a better understanding of the initiative and how it is being designed or has been designed.

*Target Population, Participant Selection, and Other Stakeholders*

- Who is the target population for this initiative (for example, high-potential early managers, organizational executives, or human resource managers)?
- Why do these individuals need a development initiative? Why does this initiative focus on them in particular?
- What is the selection process to participate?
- Does the selection process make sense in light of the overall target population and initiative goals?
- What are relevant practices and policies related to this initiative?
- How do the participants view this particular initiative? What positive and negative associations does it have from their perspective?
- Who are other stakeholders involved in the development process?
- How do the stakeholders view this particular initiative? What positive and negative associations does it have from their perspective?

*Design Elements*

- Is the initiative based on a particular leadership framework or competency model?

**Exhibit 2.2 – Understanding the Initiative Design** (continued)

- What content will be delivered and how will it be delivered?
- How will participants engage in the initiative, and over what span of time? Will it include virtual components?
- Are there plans to develop or change the initiative over time?

*Barriers and Supports*

- How will learning transfer be supported? What role will managers play in supporting participants in their development? What type of organizational supports may be needed to enhance learning transfer?
- What barriers might get in the way of participants applying what they learn?
- To what extent and how will participants and their managers be held accountable for their development as a result of the initiative?

*Existing Data Sources*

- What data will be collected during the initiative that may be useful in an evaluation? What data are being collected by other groups or departments that may be useful in an evaluation? What evaluation techniques, such as end-of-initiative surveys, are already designed for or in use by the initiative?
- What assessment instruments will the initiative use that could also be used to measure change during the evaluation?

## Create a Results Framework

Once the desired results of the initiative have been clearly articulated and the initiative has been designed (or at least an initial design has been proposed), different tools and processes can be applied to assess whether the design is likely to achieve the desired results. We recommend mapping the initiative to expected outcomes in a results framework. Similar approaches and tools to show these connections are referred to as a *results model*, *logic model*, *theory of change*, or *pathway map* (see, for example, Chapter Two in Hannum, Martineau, & Reinelt, 2007, or Martineau & Patterson, 2010).

Asking key stakeholders to help develop or review the results framework for your initiative can create valuable dialogue and alignment around the purpose of the initiative. It can ensure that designs are based on logical connections to and theory about what will actually work versus what is the most exciting or innovative development activity at the time. For example, a designer who has just had a great experience with a newly developed simulation may have a bias toward incorporating that into every initiative, even when it isn't aligned with initiative goals. Similarly, it can help designers identify gaps in an initiative and make adjustments as necessary. You can learn more about logic modeling on the W. K. Kellogg Foundation website: http://www.wkkf.org/resource-directory/resource/2006/02/wk-kellogg-foundation-logic-model-development-guide.

Whatever approach you choose to use, it is important to make sure the purpose of the initiative and the evaluation are clear from the perspective of key stakeholders. One way to do that is to create a leadership-development results framework like the one in Table 2.2 below. This type of results framework can be used to check your understanding of the intended results and to engage stakeholders in discussions that lead to common understanding and agreement about the intended outcomes of the initiative.

The framework outlines common areas to examine as part of an evaluation and is organized by the type of information that would be gathered. The areas listed are intended to spark ideas for what you might include in a similar framework customized for your situation; they reflect what we tend to examine in our own practice as well as what we've seen frequently in the literature. That said, this is not a comprehensive list. The following provides an explanation of what to include in each of the sections of our sample results map.

**Needs assessment.** The needs-assessment column focuses on information that is gathered as part of or prior to the design of a leadership-development initiative or process. The focus of the evaluation at this stage is to gather data about the context of and need for leadership development. This assessment should lead to a clear understanding of the business challenges and needs from the perspective of different stakeholders, the purpose of and need for leadership development, and appropriate contextual considerations including supports and barriers to an effective initiative.

**Initiative design.** The design column should include key components including elements that ensure the design is responsive to the culture and needs of the organization and the target population and how it will lead to the desired results.

Table 2.2 – Leadership Development Results Framework

| **NEEDS ASSESSMENT**<br>*Information on the context and need for the initiative* | **INITIATIVE DESIGN**<br>*Description of key design elements critical to expected results* | **INITIAL RESPONSE TO THE INITIATIVE**<br>*Data gathered shortly after or during the initiative* |
|---|---|---|
| At the minimum will include:<br><br>Organizational challenges<br><br>Development needs<br><br>Contextual factors | Clearly stated purpose aligned with organizational needs<br><br>Clearly specified outcomes<br><br>Appropriate selection and preparation of participants and other stakeholders<br><br>Adequate organizational support for implementation<br><br>Implementation fidelity | Typically includes gathering feedback from participants about their experience, perceptions of content relevance to their roles, their intention to apply what they learned, and feedback for program improvement. |
| **INTERNAL FACTORS:** supervisor support, organizational support, strategy and culture, changes in organizational structure or talent systems | | |

## Table 2.2 – Leadership Development Results Framework (continued)

| EXPECTED RESULTS<br>*Specific and measurable outcomes expected to take place as a result of the initiative* | | | |
|---|---|---|---|
| **Individual** | **Group** | **Organizational** | **Societal** |
| Outcomes related to the individual leader. This can include change in beliefs, increased knowledge, change in leadership behaviors, and ability to get better leadership results. | Outcomes related to groups. Includes shifts in collective beliefs, knowledge gain, change in interaction patterns, collective capabilities, and better group-level leadership results. | Outcomes for an entire organization. Includes shifts in collective beliefs, knowledge gain, change in interaction patterns, collective capabilities, and better group-level leadership results. | Outcomes that go beyond a single organization and extend to broader society. May include improved capabilities and better leadership results in an industry, community, country, region, or the world. |
| **EXTERNAL FACTORS:** changes in the economy, changes in competitive environment, changes in political or legal context | | | |

Initial response to the initiative. This column includes data gathered shortly after or during the leadership-development experience to document the response to the initiative and to identify areas that may require further attention (such as participants not seeing how to apply what they learned on the job).

Expected results. Results are organized into four subcolumns: individual, group, organizational, and societal. Not all initiatives will need all four columns, depending on the intended outcomes of the development. Completing these columns with stakeholder input and buy-in can be the most challenging and, at the same time, rewarding part of this process.

Contextual factors. These factors reflect conditions within or outside the organization that may not be directly related to the leadership-development initiative but are important to consider when designing the evaluation and interpreting data, as they may influence outcomes and results. Internal factors can include a recent merger, major organizational change, or a turnover of the organization's key leadership. External factors can include changes in the economy, market trends and changes, or a natural disaster.

## Determine the Evaluation Questions

Once you understand the expectations of key stakeholders and the leadership-development initiative, you can define the questions the evaluation should answer. It is important to understand the difference between evaluation questions and survey or interview questions. Evaluation questions focus on the big picture. They include critical questions about the initiative and its impact. Survey or interview questions are more detailed and are created specifically to generate data for analysis. Evaluation questions should be well defined and linked to stakeholder expectations so that they appropriately address their specific interests and concerns. Clarifying the key overarching questions linked to stakeholder expectations is a critical step to ensuring the evaluation leads to relevant and useful data, analysis, and findings.

We recommend that your evaluation address only a few key questions to keep the evaluation goals clear and to maintain a focused effort during the implementation phase.

Several specific questions related to a particular development initiative can be investigated. Those questions might include the following:

- To what extent does the leadership-development initiative meet its stated objectives?
- Are there any unintended benefits or challenges raised by the initiative?
- To what degree have participants applied what they have learned to their work?

- To what extent have participants made significant behavioral changes?
- What is the impact of participants' behavioral changes (or other changes) on those around them?
- Has the organization experienced the intended changes (benefits) as a result of the initiative?
- To what extent did the various components of the initiative contribute to impact?
- How can the initiative be strengthened to improve impact?

Prioritizing evaluation questions serves two functions. The first is to reduce the overall number of questions. If a question is not important, should resources be expended to address it? The second function is to determine the merit of the different questions. Determining what is critical to know versus what is interesting is important. There are multiple ways to prioritize evaluation questions, from having stakeholder groups vote or rate the importance, to asking funders to decide what they are willing to provide resources for. As you focus in on a narrow group of evaluation questions, consider the following: What kind of information about the impact of the initiative do various stakeholders need? What will they do with the information? Why do they need it?

This is also a good time to work with stakeholders to create an evaluative rubric. Evaluative rubrics are high-level interpretation guides for data that help evaluators provide overall assessments about the merit and worth of a program or initiative. They can be used to combine information from different sources to arrive at an evaluative judgment such as "Is the program good enough to warrant continued investment?" For example, if a primary evaluation question is "Has the organization experienced the intended changes (benefits) as a result of the initiative?" then a rubric would define or provide guidance about what level and types of change would be needed to decide if the result was excellent, good, adequate, or inadequate.

Creating a rubric is one way to help stakeholders identify what is most important to know and what evidence to consider when addressing an evaluation question. It can also help stakeholders agree on and document what "adequate performance" looks like. Having this conversation before data are collected can reveal what information, and in what form, would be most useful and important for key stakeholders. Rubrics can range from general to very specific. The sample rubric provided in Table 2.3 is general. It can be helpful to scope out a general rubric during the planning stage of the evaluation and then add more detail once more is known about data collection. You can see from the sample rubric that even a general rubric provides cues about how stakeholders define success and what kinds of data would be helpful.

## Table 2.3 – Sample Rubric

**"Has the organization experienced the intended changes (benefits) as a result of the initiative?"**

| | **Excellent** | **Good** | **Adequate** | **Inadequate** |
|---|---|---|---|---|
| Overall Rating | All sources of data show significant positive changes. | Data from some key areas as well as other sources show significant positive change. | Data from some key areas show positive change. | Little or no positive changes are found. |
| Key Areas | | | | |
| Improved Networks | Strategically important new and useful networks are developed throughout the organization. | Strategically important new and useful networks are developed across many units. | Some new and useful networks are developed across some units. | No new or useful networks are developed across units. |
| Improved Product Development | Many new product ideas, product enhancements, *and* development/delivery efficiencies are related to the program. | Many new product ideas, product enhancements, *or* development/delivery efficiencies are related to the program. | Some new product ideas, product enhancements, or development/delivery efficiencies are related to the program. | No new product ideas, product enhancements, or development/delivery efficiencies are related to the program. |

## Create an Evaluation Plan

An evaluation plan ensures (1) that the results of a development initiative are measured so that they meet the expectations of participants and other stakeholder groups and (2) helps stakeholders understand exactly what will be evaluated so they can design the development initiative to produce desired results. Organizations benefit from an evaluation plan because it clarifies what is happening, when, and why. As you plan your evaluation, be sure to indicate the relationship between specific evaluation questions, components of the leadership-development initiative, timelines, and selected evaluation methods. The evaluation plan examples that follow can serve as templates for a design that serves your particular circumstances.

Your plan provides an overview of data-collection activities and helps ensure that you are collecting the appropriate data needed to answer the evaluation questions. A good evaluation plan will include other activities, such as the communication of results (for example, what results are communicated, to whom, and by what media).

When you create your evaluation plan, you don't yet have to know the specific content for each method (for example, the questions for your survey). Your intent at this point is to choose methods that are:

- likely to produce the type of data valued by key stakeholders;
- capable of addressing each specific evaluation question;
- logistically feasible and set for an appropriate time frame; and
- appropriate for the people who will be asked to provide the data.

In developing your evaluation plan, it's important to understand the context in which the leadership development and evaluation are taking place. For example, in an organizational setting an evaluator needs to consider the ebb and flow of work and to take critical times in an organization's calendar into account. Many organizations have periods that are particularly busy and stressful—these are bad times to conduct evaluation activities if it can be avoided. For example, if the people you wish to collect survey data from are enmeshed in annual budget planning, they may not have time to complete your survey or may rush through it without providing useful data. You may be able to get more people to respond to your survey if you wait a month. Making the evaluation process as simple and convenient as possible can reduce scheduling problems and help you gather the information you need from the people you need to hear from.

Creating a budget is part of designing an evaluation; you'll want to have some idea about the amount and type of resources (money, time, and staff) available. As a general rule, evaluations typically take up 5 to 20% of the cost of a development initiative. The cost depends on the complexity of the initiative and the evaluation. The following are important questions to ask when considering the resources needed for your evaluation:

- When are stakeholders expecting to see results?
- Will you have enough support to hire professional evaluators to design and either implement or oversee the evaluation?
- Will you have access to survey software that has built-in analysis and reporting or will you need to source that yourself (if needed)?
- How much data will be collected during the evaluation? How will the organization use the evaluation results?

You will need to make resources available to collect the necessary data, analyze it, and communicate the results. If stakeholders want to measure results at multiple stages, you will need to allocate your resources appropriately to meet that need. Skill sets you may want to tap for conducting an evaluation include database experience, statistical knowledge, survey development, interviewing experience, focus-group facilitation, and project management. If the organization has available staff with these skills, that can reduce costs. Many evaluation approaches encourage stakeholders to be part of the entire evaluation process, not only as advisers but as gatherers and analyzers of information. This approach is often referred to as *participatory evaluation* and it can reduce costs and serve as a development opportunity.

Evaluation plans can be as simple or as complex as you need them to be. We've included a few examples in Tables 2.4 and 2.5 to illustrate the different ways information can be displayed.

Once you have taken these initial steps, you have laid the foundation for planning the evaluation. You are now ready to get more specific about the evaluation plan and flesh out the methods that will be used. The next chapter provides an overview of commonly used methods and approaches to evaluating leadership-development initiatives.

## Table 2.4 – Evaluation Plan Example 1
### Longitudinal Outcome Evaluation for the ABC Leadership Development Program

| Evaluation Questions | Time Frame and Data-Collection Methods (Source*) | | | |
|---|---|---|---|---|
| | **January** | **April** | **August** | **November** |
| Were learning objectives met? | Survey (P) | | | |
| How do participants intend to apply their learning and new skills? | Survey (P) | | | |
| Is there growth in competencies? | | 360-degree behavioral change instrument (P, M, DR, Pe, O) | | |
| Are participants receiving support for development and application of new competencies? | | Survey (P); Interviews (P) | | Survey (P); Interviews (P) |
| What changes are resulting in participants' work groups? | | | Survey (P, M); Interviews (P, M) | |
| How is the organization benefiting? | | | | Analysis of organizational data (C) |
| Communication Timeline | February: mini summary (S, C) | June: 360-degree reports (P); July: interim report (S, C) | September: mini summary (S, C) | January: final, comprehensive report (S, C), debriefing |

***Data Source Key**
P = participant (individual, group, or team)
Pe = peer of participant
M = manager of participant
O = other (client, customer, etc.)
DR = direct report of participant
C = key organizational client contact

### Table 2.5 – Evaluation Plan Example 2
Pilot and Ongoing Implementation and Outcome Evaluation of the MNQ Leadership Development Program

| | Questions | Data-Collection Timing | Participants | Trainers | Coordi-nators | Sales Staff |
|---|---|---|---|---|---|---|
| PILOT PHASE ONLY | How effective is the current logistical support? How well are program processes (advance information for participants, test administration process, program setup, etc.) functioning in the multiple locations? | during and immediately after the program | | program debrief | program debrief | |
| | Do program staff and faculty have the information and resources they need to provide the highest-quality program? What's helpful? What's missing? | during and immediately after the program | | program debrief | program debrief | |
| | Why do participants select this program? What appeals to them about the program? What doesn't appeal to them? | | focus groups | | | focus groups |
| | Is the flow of the program logical and helpful to participants? | immediately after the program | focus groups | program debrief | program debrief | |
| | Are all aspects of the program functioning as intended (in order to meet objectives)? | immediately after the program | | | | |

(continued)

| Questions | Data-Collection Timing | Participants | Trainers | Coordi-nators | Sales Staff |
|---|---|---|---|---|---|
| Pilot Phase Communication Plan:<br>• written report and presentation to program design team (including trainers) two weeks after the program;<br>• tailored summary of lessons learned to sales staff one or two days after presentation to program design team;<br>• tailored summaries of lessons learned to participants and coordinators one month after the program | | | | | |
| To what extent does the program meet the stated objectives? | immediately after the program | end-of-program survey | | | |
| To what extent are the program objectives relevant? | immediately after the program | end-of-program survey | | | |
| What are the changes in the selected competencies? | three months after the program | 360-degree retrospective pre/post survey | | | |
| What is the impact on the participants' organizations? | three months and six months after the program | 360-degree retrospective pre/post survey and impact survey | | | |

*(continued)*

Table 2.5 – Evaluation Plan Example 2

Pilot and Ongoing Implementation and Outcome Evaluation of the MNQ Leadership Development Program (continued)

PROCESS

| Questions | Data-Collection Timing | Participants | Trainers | Coordi-nators | Sales Staff |
|---|---|---|---|---|---|
| Are there any unintended consequences of the program? | six months after the program | interviews | | | |
| What are the barriers and supports for making changes? | six months after the program | interviews | | | |
| Ongoing Communication Plan:<br>• end-of-program survey to trainers and coordinators immediately;<br>• quarterly summary reports of end-of-program survey data to program manager;<br>• individual 360-degree reports to participants the day after data-collection deadline;<br>• semiannual aggregate 360-degree report to program manager;<br>• semiannual impact survey report to program manager | | | | | |

## Checklist – Chapter Two

### Gather Information, Plan, and Conceptualize the Evaluation

- ✓ Plan your evaluation when the development initiative is being designed.
- ✓ Identify and engage stakeholders with an interest in the initiative and its evaluation.
- ✓ Surface expectations and define purpose of the initiative.
- ✓ Understand the initiative design, including the types of impact the initiative is expected to have, its target audience, and the period of time over which the impact is expected to occur.
- ✓ Create a results framework.
- ✓ Determine and prioritize evaluation questions.
- ✓ Create an evaluative rubric.
- ✓ Create an evaluation plan that includes data-collection methods, resources for the evaluation, and how the evaluation results will be used.

# CHAPTER THREE
## Collect and Analyze Data

After you have focused the evaluation and developed the evaluation plan, you are ready to conduct the evaluation, which is where data collection and analysis become key concerns. In this chapter, we provide you with concrete examples of data-collection approaches. As you think through data collection, keep in mind the importance of maintaining confidentiality of individual data. Confidentiality can build evaluator credibility and create trust that the process will be used to evaluate the initiative, not the individual. Individual data should not be shared with anyone unless that individual gives permission to share the data with other specific people. Individuals (and their observers) will often be more candid and honest in their responses when they know their data will not be shared with others except in aggregate form. Confidentiality can mean different things to different people, so you need to be clear about how information will be shared and with whom.

There are many tools and techniques evaluators can use to gather data (Hoole & Martineau, 2014). The challenge and goal for evaluators is to select the appropriate tools and techniques to efficiently and effectively fulfill the purposes of the evaluation. In the following sections we describe several techniques that are particularly relevant to evaluating leadership-development initiatives. Descriptions, examples, and advice to help you learn more about various data-collection methods are included, as are tips related to each method. Most, if not all, of these methods are useful for evaluating many different types of initiatives as well. We recognize that there are other methods that evaluators and practitioners use for evaluating leadership-development initiatives that are fantastic and can be a perfect fit for a particular need, in a particular context. We decided to focus on what we use most often in our practice and what we see frequently in the literature, rather than try to describe all possible approaches. What is important is that you identify the methods that will produce the type of data your stakeholders expect, in the time frame they expect it, and that you collect data in a way that is accepted by all of your stakeholders.

As you consider different methods you will also need to think about tools for gathering the data (for example, What kind of survey will be used and how will it be administered?) and storing your data (for example, Do you have access to a secure, relational database?). Do you have the resources to fully implement and use the data from the methods you have selected? For instance, if you are gathering interview data, do you have the resources to transcribe and code the interviews? Do you have the resources to analyze workplace statistics in an appropriate manner?

The following questions will help you think through possible approaches that you might take. Select those data-collection methods that have the best chance of getting the information you need to carry out an effective evaluation.

## Which Methods Are Best Suited for Answering Your Evaluation Questions?

Both qualitative and quantitative data can be collected from different methods. However, some evaluation questions are better answered with one or the other type of data. If your question asks how often or how much, a quantitative approach, such as a survey or an assessment instrument that gathers frequencies or percentages, would be appropriate. But if your question asks in what ways or how, a qualitative approach, such as face-to-face interviews or focus groups, might be a more effective data-collection method. Many evaluation questions are best answered with a mix of qualitative and quantitative data. For example, it is helpful to have participants give feedback on a program in a survey with easily tallied and presented quantitative data (for instance, rating level of satisfaction or likelihood to recommend the program to others) and complementary qualitative data (for instance, examples of how they plan to apply what they learned and suggestions for improvement). A focus group could be used to collect more-in-depth qualitative data on new programs in order to understand specific reactions to particular components of the program and to contribute to a deeper understanding of how to improve the program. Quantitative organizational data may be used to determine impact (for instance, retention or promotion rates), and qualitative data from those who experienced the improvements will help make clear connections between the statistics and the initiative.

## What Is the Purpose of Your Evaluation? Who Will Use the Information, and How Will They Use It?

Evaluations typically seek to provide evidence or information related to one or more areas (refer to the list at the beginning of Chapter One). What kind of information is best suited for the purpose? Do you need to prove the value of the initiative or tell the story of impact from different perspectives? Once you have a clear purpose in mind, consider how and who will use the information you intend to gather. Because different kinds of data lead to different kinds of understanding, it's important for you to think about how useful certain kinds of data will be as stakeholders look toward putting results into action. But be careful not to allow the preference of any stakeholder group to mandate what data you collect and how. Understanding stakeholder preferences is important, but the methods you choose should always be appropriate for the evaluation question you seek to answer.

## What Motivated the Need to Evaluate in the First Place?

If the goal of your evaluation is to gather information from many individuals, a quantitative method (such as a survey) might be the most efficient and cost-effective method. But if the purpose is to understand the complexities of a situation (to get more-in-depth information), qualitative methods such as face-to-face interviews or focus groups are more effective. Your evaluation may need both kinds of data and benefit from a mixed-method approach.

### How Practical and Feasible Is Each Method?

The practicality and feasibility of a method often boils down to a few central issues: cost, amount of data needed, time frame for the work, the amount of burden on data sources, and resources needed to analyze and use data. If you must conduct your evaluation quickly and assess a large number of people using limited resources, it might be best to use a quantitative method such as a survey or assessment instrument. If you have enough time and resources (both technological and human), you can reasonably choose from qualitative methods such as observation, telephone and face-to-face interviews, and focus groups. In addition to financial resources and time constraints, give careful consideration to the practicality and feasibility of using different approaches given the evaluation expertise available to you (data collection, management, analysis, and interpretation). For instance, if you plan to use interviewing as one of your data-collection techniques, how will you analyze that information? If you plan to collect survey data, how will you analyze and present the results?

Creating an evaluation plan that links your evaluation questions with your data-collection techniques (see the evaluation plan examples in Chapter Two) is a useful strategy for developing a comprehensive and well-documented evaluation plan. Although it takes additional effort at the beginning of the evaluation project, it typically saves time (as well as confusion and disappointment) in the long run.

## Overview of Approaches

The advantages and disadvantages of different data-collection approaches will vary based on the specific tool being used and the context in which it is applied. However, at a general level there are basic considerations as well as advantages and disadvantages that can be helpful to consider when deciding on an approach. These are outlined in the following table. More detailed information about each approach is provided after the table.

## Pilot Testing Data-Collection Tools

A pilot test can act as a dress rehearsal for your evaluation. It entails testing aspects of your evaluation (for instance, survey instruments, interview protocols) with a small group of people in advance of launching it more widely. A pilot test has several benefits. You can determine whether responses seem appropriate, interview protocols can be tested to ensure that questions are clear and are eliciting intended responses, and surveys can be tested to see whether the questions are clearly written and the response options make sense. It can reveal unforeseen shortcomings in data-collection tools and help you hone your collection process and analysis strategies.

Ideally, your pilot test would include an analysis of the data to determine whether the measure is properly designed to deliver the desired kind of information. Doing this would allow you to provide a mock report to share with stakeholders to ensure the evaluation will provide data that is considered valuable and useful. Ideally, the sample size of your pilot test should be similar to the intended sample size of the actual evaluation. However, in practice, you may have to work with a

## Table 3.1 – Advantages and Disadvantages of Data-Collection Approaches

| Method | Considerations | Advantages | Disadvantages |
|---|---|---|---|
| Surveys | Use an existing survey or create a new one?<br><br>Online or paper administration?<br><br>If online, what survey software?<br><br>How long and what type of survey is feasible? | Good for collecting quantitative data and measuring change.<br><br>Easy to track data over time and across cohorts.<br><br>Easy to administer.<br><br>Can collect data from a large number of people efficiently.<br><br>Administration and reporting software is readily available and often inexpensive.<br><br>Can be fully confidential or anonymous. | May require internet access.<br><br>Response rates may be low. Advanced analysis skills may be needed.<br><br>Doesn't easily allow for changes to questions or follow-up questions for clarification. |
| Interviews | Use internal or external interviewers?<br><br>Face-to-face or virtual?<br><br>Use the same questions for everyone or allow for "in the moment" follow-up? | Good for collecting rich qualitative data.<br><br>Can probe for clarification, explanations, and examples.<br><br>Can be fully confidential. | Data collection and analysis can be time-consuming and more expensive than a survey.<br><br>Can require more time commitment from interviewee.<br><br>Need a skilled interviewer.<br><br>More difficult to collect data from a large number of people in a short time.<br><br>Cannot be anonymous.<br><br>*(continued)* |

## Table 3.1 – Advantages and Disadvantages of Data-Collection Approaches (continued)

| Method | Considerations | Advantages | Disadvantages |
|---|---|---|---|
| Focus Groups | How many people in each focus group?<br><br>Face-to-face or virtual?<br><br>If face-to-face, where should the focus group be held?<br><br>What is the best way to record/ document the focus group? | Good for collecting rich qualitative data.<br><br>More efficient than collecting individual interviews.<br><br>Can probe for clarification, explanations, and examples. | Data collection and analysis can be time-consuming.<br><br>More challenging than other methods to collect virtually.<br><br>Typically more expensive than surveys.<br><br>Need a skilled facilitator.<br><br>Difficult to identify individual responses.<br><br>Not fully confidential or anonymous. |
| Archival Documents and Data | Can you get access to the data when needed?<br><br>Do data provide the right kind of information?<br><br>Are data in a format you can use? | Can simplify data collection.<br><br>Typically lower cost than other options.<br><br>Reduced burden on participants. | Data may not be available when needed.<br><br>Data may not measure what is truly needed or may not measure it in a highly useable fashion.<br><br>Data may not be in an easily useable format.<br><br>Can be time-consuming to sift through data looking for themes or relevant information. |

*(continued)*

## Table 3.1 – Advantages and Disadvantages of Data-Collection Approaches (continued)

| Method | Considerations | Advantages | Disadvantages |
|---|---|---|---|
| Work-place Statistics | Can you get access to the data when needed?<br><br>Do data provide the right kind of information?<br><br>Are data in a format you can use? | Can simplify data collection.<br><br>Typically lower cost than other options.<br><br>Reduced burden on participants. | Data may not be available or accessible when needed.<br><br>Data may not measure what is needed or may not measure it in a useful fashion.<br><br>Changes in data may be due to other factors.<br><br>Sifting through data looking for themes or relevant information can be time-consuming. |
| Observa-tions | Will you observe in the organiza-tional context or in a simulated environment?<br><br>Will observers record what they see as desired or follow a strict protocol? | Data on behaviors collected in a natural context.<br><br>Can provide detailed examples of behaviors. | Requires well-trained observers.<br><br>Can be time-consuming to collect data.<br><br>More expensive.<br><br>May alter behavior, knowing they are being observed.<br><br>Can be disruptive to the workplace.<br><br>*(continued)* |

Table 3.1 – Advantages and Disadvantages of Data-Collection Approaches (continued)

| Method | Considerations | Advantages | Disadvantages |
|---|---|---|---|
| Projective Techniques (for example, Photovoice or Visual Explorer) | How will data be documented or recorded?<br><br>Are additional tools needed? | Often more engaging than traditional methods.<br><br>Can be used to supplement or enhance interviews or focus groups.<br><br>May prompt deeper levels of information. | Often not robust enough to be used as a standalone evaluation method.<br><br>Requires a skilled facilitator.<br><br>Often are not confidential.<br><br>May require additional resources (for example, a camera or visual aids). |

much smaller sample because you can't reuse pilot data and you need to leave an adequate sample for your formal evaluation.

You may not have the time, resources, or opportunity to conduct a pilot test. An alternative way to ensure that you will collect good information is to form a data-collection review team. This team can review any surveys or protocols you develop for use in data collection and examine the process and analysis strategies you intend to employ. Members of the team might include subject-matter experts (people who know about the content area you are measuring), technical or measurement experts (people who know about measurement methods and research), population-group experts (people familiar with the target population), and experts in the effects of bias, ethics, and similarly affective issues. Including stakeholders in the instrument-review process can be a way to build their engagement with and commitment to the evaluation work while providing information that strengthens the evaluation.

## Surveys

**General development and use.** Surveys are frequently used to collect information from a large number of individuals on a broad range of subjects. Surveys prompt respondents to answer questions or rate information about demographics, knowledge, opinions, feelings, perspectives, or behaviors. The increased availability of online-survey software has made it relatively easy to create and distribute surveys quickly, but survey creation, designs, cost, and reporting are still a complex process. Several types of surveys and survey approaches will be discussed in this chapter, such as daily evaluation surveys, end-of-initiative surveys, and surveys that assess learning or change. But before getting into the details, we address issues related to surveys generally.

**Reliability and validity.** Whether you use or adapt an existing evaluation instrument like a survey or decide to develop a new one, paying attention to the quality and consistency of the data collected and exploring what results mean and how they are used are important parts of the evaluation process; understanding the reliability and validity associated with what you aim to assess with a survey is central to that process. In general, *reliability* is the consistency of data from an assessment, and *validity* is the accuracy of data from an assessment and the appropriateness of using those assessment data for a specific purpose. Neither reliability nor validity can be measured absolutely or established definitively for an assessment because they are characteristics of the data and how they are used and are not a characteristic of the assessment.

Reliability is the degree to which an assessment produces consistent results. If an assessment does not produce consistent scores, you may be getting more error than information about how that individual is actually performing or thinking. Reliability is never truly measured, but it can be estimated. The same test will likely have different reliability estimates depending on how it is calculated and the sample used. The appropriate reliability level depends on the situation. Statistical measures of reliability (for instance, Cronbach's alpha) are usually reported on a scale ranging from 0 to 1, with estimates closer to 1 being preferred.

There are three ways commonly used to assess reliability. *Internal consistency* provides information about whether questions on a scale are measuring the same concept. *Interrater agreement* provides information about the degree to which ratings from different sources agree. *Test-retest* provides information about the stability of questions and scales over time.

Validity is the combination of two ideas: the degree to which an assessment measures what it claims to measure and the usefulness and appropriateness of using those assessment data for a given purpose. Validity is an extremely important consideration when you are developing or using surveys. Validity is a multifaceted concept, and multiple types of evidence are needed to establish it. Evidence should be gathered in the varying situations and with the different populations for which the assessment is intended. Validity has to do with the content of the test, the people taking the test, the purpose of the test, and the consequences of the test.

There are several types of validity evidence:

- *Content validity* is the extent to which assessment adequately and comprehensively measures what it claims to measure.
- *Construct validity* is carried in the relationship between the survey content and the constructs it is intended to measure. Typically, this type of evidence involves logical or empirical analysis, including statistical comparisons to other assessments and expert judgments of the relationship between the assessment and the construct.
- *Criterion validity* is found in the relationship between the assessment and a criterion such as effective performance. Consider, for example, the connection between an assessment of job performance and job-performance ratings.
- *Concurrent evidence* refers to evidence collected at the time the test is administered, and *predictive evidence* is evidence collected at a later time.
- *Consequential validity* refers to the social and cultural consequences of assessment use. If there is an unintended negative impact resulting from using an assessment that was developed for one group with another group, that would be an example of a negative consequence. In other words, an assessment developed for and delivered to a company in the United States might be perceived differently by participants from other parts of the world. If the scores or ratings were different in some way that did not have to do with what was being measured, then rewards or punitive measures based on those scores would not be a valid use of those data.

We sometimes take for granted that an assessment is providing accurate, useful, and appropriate information. Assessments do not always do that. Validity studies are one way that question or test bias or unfairness can be revealed. *Bias* is the presence of a question or test characteristic that results in differential performance for individuals of the same ability but from different ethnic, gender, cultural, social status, or religious groups. Bias often stems from limitations of our perspective and understanding. No survey is free from bias, but question and test bias and unfairness can be detected and reduced by considering the test with a lens toward cultural competence. In other words, having different experts who have specific knowledge of the people and place in which the survey will be used might help to uncover some items that are culturally insensitive or offensive before the assessment administration.

Although you can gather useful and valuable information through surveys without formal testing for reliability and validity, the more you pay attention to developing valid and reliable instruments, the more confident you can be in your findings. As with evaluation design in general, there are trade-offs to be made in determining how much to test instruments before using them. Ultimately, validity and reliability will help in increasing the trustworthiness of the data collected from instruments used in an evaluation. Investing in reliability and validity studies can increase the consistency and accuracy of the measures used in an evaluation.

**Guidelines for developing a survey.** Although commonly used, a survey is one of the most challenging instruments to develop well. When designed in haste, surveys often collect inaccurate and useless information. As you consider developing one or more surveys, consider some of the following advice:

- Map survey sections and items to the overarching evaluation questions to help identify which constructs are over- or underemphasized within the survey instrument.
- Decide on the sample that needs to complete the survey. For example, does everyone in a group need to complete the survey or would a random or purposeful sampling approach work well?
- Determine how the survey can best be administered. If online survey administration makes the most sense, identify what features are most important such as specific item types, reporting options, language capability, devices supported, and data export and storage options.
- If appropriate, add dynamic elements such as skip logic, personalized text substitution, and multimedia embedding into online surveys to make the experience of the respondent more engaging and the collection of data more efficient.

Before you begin the question-writing process, clearly identify the areas you want to assess. Select representative behaviors, skills, and competencies. Relate them to the initiative and prioritize them. Then determine the type of information you need to capture. For example, you may need to collect data related to the frequency of a specific behavior or related to the evidence that a defined skill level has been attained. This process will help you write survey questions that are specific and relevant to your evaluation. Your next step is to create a survey blueprint that organizes the questions according to the type of information you plan to capture. See the example below.

### Exhibit 3.1 – Sample Survey Blueprint

| Type of Information Collected | Survey Question |
|---|---|
| Satisfaction with Coaching | • Please indicate your level of satisfaction with your executive coaching experience to date. (1 = *Not at all satisfied at all* to 5 = *Extremely satisfied*) |
| Commitment of Coachee | • How committed are you personally to the coaching process? (Committed means you were motivated to put time and energy into your development by making time for the coaching calls, listening deeply to the feedback you received, and taking follow-up actions based upon the coaching.) (1 = *Not at all committed* to 5 = *Very committed*) |
| Quality of Coaching | • Provide an overall quality rating of your coach. (1 = *Low quality* to 5 = *Very high quality*) |
| Coaching Process | • Please rate your level of agreement with the following statements: (1 = *Strongly disagree* to 5 = *Strongly agree*)<br>a. My coach clarified the purpose of the coaching relationship.<br>b. My coach follows through on agreements.<br>c. My coach helped me recognize my current strengths.<br>d. My coach assisted me in recognizing areas for improvement.<br>e. My coach encourages new ways of thinking.<br>f. My coach encourages me to practice new behaviors.<br>g. My coach is knowledgeable about business practices/organizational issues. |
| Progress on Goals | • What are your top 3 development areas/goals? (*3 open-ended fields*)<br>• To what extent have you made progress on your development goals (*answers from previous question piped to this question*)? (1 = *No extent* to 5 = *Very great extent*)<br>• To what extent has the coaching experience helped you make progress toward solving current organizational challenges you face? (1 = *No extent* to 5 = *Very great extent*) |

**Exhibit 3.1 – Sample Survey Blueprint** (continued)

| Type of Information Collected | Survey Question |
|---|---|
| Coachee Feedback/ Challenges Faced in Coaching Process | Please provide comments regarding your current coaching experience, including what is working well and what could be done to make the experience better. |
| Manager Support | • Please rate your level of agreement with the following statements: (*1 = Strongly disagree* to *5 = Strongly agree*)<br>a. My manager met with me prior to or at the beginning of the executive-coaching process to discuss my development goals.<br>b. My manager met with me to review the development plan I created.<br>c. My manager has supported me in my development process. |
| Readiness for Coaching | • Please rate your level of agreement with the following statements: (*1 = Strongly disagree* to *5 = Strongly agree*)<br>a. Self-improvement and personal growth are a priority for me.<br>b. I am motivated to put time and energy into my development.<br>c. I feel fully prepared for career advancement.<br>d. I am willing to work outside of my comfort zone.<br>e. I am open to and welcome the contributions of others.<br>f. I am open to new concepts and out-of-the-box ideas and approaches. |

*(continued)*

**Exhibit 3.1 – Sample Survey Blueprint** (continued)

*Things to Do When Writing Survey Questions*

- Be as concise as possible without losing the meaning of the question.
- Write questions at approximately an 8th-grade reading level.
- Use specific language with common meaning and interpretation.
- Create several questions to measure complex phenomena.
- Consider including open-ended questions that ask for specific information.

*Things Not to Do When Writing Survey Questions*

- Don't use colloquialisms, metaphors, similes, figures of speech, culturally biased phrases, scientific words, or jargon.
- Don't be unnecessarily wordy.
- Don't use double negatives.
- Don't use inflammatory or derogatory language.
- Don't attempt to measure several ideas in a single question.

## Increasing Response Rates

A response rate is the percentage of individuals who complete a data-collection activity versus the number invited to participate. So if you send a survey to 100 people and 30 people return a completed survey, your response rate is 30%. In some evaluations you may identify a "sample" or subgroup of people, such as participants, to respond to a survey. If there are a total of 500 participants and you decide to randomly select 100 for your survey and 50 respond, you have a 50% response rate, even though you were only receiving completed surveys from 10% of all participants. Encouraging people to respond to a survey, or any other request to provide information for that matter, can be hard, especially when they don't have to. Below are a few things we recommend.

- **Let people know a request is coming.** If you know you will be gathering data from initiative participants, for instance, let them know during the initiative that they will be contacted after the initiative. Explain why participating in the process is important and how information will be used. If there are benefits to them for participating in the process, take the time during the initiative to explain the benefits and to answer questions.

- **Personalize your request to participate.** Send your request to the person, not their role (for instance, "Dear Kelly" rather than "Dear Participant"). It can also be helpful to have the request come from someone known by the people you are trying to get to participate (for instance, the president of the foundation or a trainer rather than an evaluator they have never met or heard of).

- **Clearly state the purpose and benefit.** In short, let them know how you will use the information and why their perspectives are important.

- **Keep your invitation short and simple.** Tell them how long it will take to complete the survey, how the information will be used, and with whom the information will be shared. Then thank them for their time.

*(continued)*

- **Remind people to complete the process.** It is important to remind people to complete data collection but not to hassle them. Usually about two reminder e-mails will be enough. Whenever possible, only remind people who have not yet completed the process.

- **Consider offering incentives.** These incentives can be a small token, gift certificate, a day off, and so on. If funds are limited you can use a raffle approach in which those completing the survey, or other data-collection effort, are entered into a drawing for a prize. In some cases the "prize" can be a donation to a cause people support. This can be done by a statement like "We will donate $1 to Charity X for every completed survey" or by an appeal for a minimum response: "If 100 people complete the survey, we will donate $500 to Charity X."

- **Offer to share aggregate results with participants.** People who respond may want to see the final results. Offering to send them this, if appropriate, can boost their participation. If reading results isn't likely to encourage individuals, you could host a community meeting to share insights or have a special presentation (in person or online) to share information and perhaps answer questions.

Now that you know more about the basics of survey development, we'll describe various kinds of surveys that are commonly used to evaluate leadership development.

End-of-initiative survey. Participants complete end-of-initiative evaluation forms at the conclusion of each component of the leadership-development initiative. You can design these forms to capture the extent to which a specific component met its target objectives, how participants intend to apply what they've learned in the workplace, and how well facilitators, facilities, and logistics met a specified standard. Use these forms for gathering evidence about how participants intend to use lessons learned, for collecting impressions of how relevant and valuable the initiative is to potential participants, and for capturing suggestions for changing the initiative. Capturing this information while it is fresh on the minds of participants is helpful, but this method doesn't measure the actual implementation of the intended changes—only the intent to apply what has been learned. See Exhibit 3.2 for an example evaluation.

***Advice:***

- Only ask for information you need at that point in time or about that point in time. Remember that participants may not have had an opportunity to apply what they have learned, so the most you can hope to know about is their intent to use what they have learned.
- If the end of the initiative is a face-to-face event, you may want to ask participants to complete the survey before they leave the event. Response rates are usually higher if you give participants the time to complete the form on-site. On the

## Exhibit 3.2 – Leadership Development Program Evaluation

Your Name: ______________________ Date: ______________________

### Overall Satisfaction:

Please use the following scale to rate the extent to which you are satisfied with the program:

1=Not at all 2=To a little extent 3=To some extent 4=To a great extent 5=To a very great extent

| | *Not at all* — *Very great extent* |
|---|---|
| Please rate your overall satisfaction with the program. | 1 2 3 4 5 |

Please comment on any aspect of your program experience that you found particularly *helpful.*

Please comment on any aspect of your program experience that you would like to see *changed.*

### Program Learning Objectives:

Please use the following scale to (1) indicate the extent to which each program objective is relevant and (2) indicate to what extent each program objective was achieved.

**As a result of this program I am better able to . . .**

| | *Not at all* — *Very great extent*<br>This objective is **relevant.** | *Not at all* — *Very great extent*<br>This objective was **achieved.** |
|---|---|---|
| Be more proactive in focusing on the challenges and concerns of different groups within the organization. | 1 2 3 4 5 | 1 2 3 4 5 |
| Utilize tools and techniques to more effectively build resiliency. | 1 2 3 4 5 | 1 2 3 4 5 |
| Deliver effective feedback. | 1 2 3 4 5 | 1 2 3 4 5 |
| Tailor communication to the audience, situation, and my personal leadership style. | 1 2 3 4 5 | 1 2 3 4 5 |
| Identify my strengths and weaknesses and have a plan to address them as necessary. | 1 2 3 4 5 | 1 2 3 4 5 |
| Solicit and utilize feedback from a variety of sources. | 1 2 3 4 5 | 1 2 3 4 5 |

other hand, participants may be tired and would provide more thoughtful and complete responses if they could complete the survey later. If you do this, you need to be willing to work with lower response rates (less than 50%) in many cases.

- If there are numerous open-ended questions, you may want to consider administering the survey electronically to avoid having to retype responses.
- Consider whether you want participants to put their names on the form. They may be more comfortable being frank if they do not have to give a name. However, you would not be able to link the information from the survey to any other information from that person, and you will not be able to follow up with someone for further clarification or to address a specific issue they raise.
- If the initiative has multiple cohorts, you may want to communicate information about what went well or poorly to the staff for the next cohort so they can make changes if needed.

**Daily evaluation survey.** In some leadership-development initiatives, participants complete evaluation forms at the end of each day (see Exhibit 3.3 for an example form). The value in these forms is twofold. First, they give participants an opportunity to reflect on their daily experiences, which reinforces what they've learned (especially when questions are written in a way that requires such reflection). Second, they provide staff with information that enables them to make any immediate necessary adjustments to the initiative, thereby enhancing its effectiveness. This method is somewhat limited in that it does not offer participants much time to reflect on their experiences and may not provide a comprehensive picture of the experience. We find it most helpful to use in a pilot or first run of a program when feedback on each part of the program can be especially helpful.

*Advice:*

- Keep your form as short as possible; participants are usually tired at the end of the day.
- Only ask for information you need at that point in time and about what happened that day. In some cases it can be helpful to first determine what information staff will actually be able to use—what immediate changes are truly realistic.
- You can use a paper or an electronic format to gather data. If you use paper, make sure to have a few extra copies on hand and writing utensils for participants to use. An electronic approach will require enough computer stations or hand-held devices for each participant. At CCL we sometimes ask participants to "bring your own device" (for instance a smartphone) that they can use to complete evaluation surveys during the program.
- Consider whether you want participants to put their names on the form. They may be more comfortable being frank if they do not have to give a name. However, you would not be able to link the information from the survey to any other information from that person, and you will not be able to follow up with someone for further clarification or to address a specific issue they raise.
- For the data to be helpful in the moment, you may want to schedule time at the end of the day to review the forms and communicate information to initiative staff (verbally or through a very short summary highlighting any concerns or anything that went particularly well).

## Exhibit 3.3 – Daily Evaluation Survey

The daily-evaluation process is designed to provide a source of reflection for you and provide the staff with feedback about the program. Your candid responses are important and appreciated, especially your additional written comments.

| 1 = *Not at all* | 2 = To a *little* extent | 3 = To *some* extent | 4 = To a *great* extent | 5 = To a *very great* extent |
|---|---|---|---|---|

# Today's Experience

| | *Not at all* | | | | *Very great* |
|---|---|---|---|---|---|
| Please rate the day in terms of its learning value. | 1 | 2 | 3 | 4 | 5 |
| Please rate the day in terms of its job relevance. | 1 | 2 | 3 | 4 | 5 |

What was your greatest learning today? Why?

______________________________

______________________________

| Which components contributed most to your learning? | *Not at all* | | | | *Very great* |
|---|---|---|---|---|---|
| Communicating your vision | 1 | 2 | 3 | 4 | 5 |
| Mind mapping | 1 | 2 | 3 | 4 | 5 |
| Facilitated group discussion | 1 | 2 | 3 | 4 | 5 |
| Other: ______________________ | 1 | 2 | 3 | 4 | 5 |

What was missing from today's session for you?

______________________________

______________________________

What do you want the faculty to do differently tomorrow?

______________________________

______________________________

What recommendations do you have to improve the day?

______________________________

______________________________

Learning surveys. Surveys (such as Exhibit 3.4 below) can be used to assess the extent to which participants have learned new content during the initiative. This method is valuable when participants are expected to retain factual information (such as their organization's leadership or competency models or its business policies or practices) or learn specific steps for implementing leadership responsibilities (such as giving feedback and coaching others). The results can be used to provide recommendations for which components need more attention—where learning did not reach the intended levels.

There are generally two ways to assess the attainment of factual information: (1) to administer the learning survey twice, once before the initiative and once immediately afterward, and (2) to administer a survey after an initiative. The first approach has two advantages over the latter. The pretest, a survey before the initiative, provides a means of assessing the needs of participants: This can guide you in focusing the measures you will use in the evaluation. This approach also allows you to create a logical tie to what has been learned with the initiative. In either case, questions must be related to the content of the initiative in order to be an accurate measure of what participants learned.

**Exhibit 3.4 – Sample Questions from Learning Survey**

In a leadership context, the acronym DAC stands for:

- Direction, Alignment, Commitment
- Diversity, Authenticity, Competence
- Direction, Accountability, Collaboration
- Development, Action, Complexity
- Director, Assistant, Coworkers

The top three components of effective feedback as described in the program are:

- Communication, Trust, Commitment
- Transparency, Collaboration, Results
- Alignment, Execution, Focus
- Situation, Behavior, Impact
- Direction, Communication, Outcomes

Understanding a colleague's interpersonal preferences is important to:

- Optimize your communication and working relationship
- Avoid pitfalls and all conflict
- Consider interpersonal differences with your personal values
- Appreciate the motivation underlying another's behavior
- All of the above

What are the three fundamental psychological needs that each individual has?

- Belonging, Autonomy, Respect
- Caring, Understanding, Aspiring
- Inclusion, Control, and Affection
- Beliefs, Behavior, Trust
- Direction, Faith, Affirmation

What are the eight competencies necessary for leadership success in ABC Organization (list all eight)?

What are the primary ways in which leaders fail at ABC Organization? (list the top three)?

How are ABC Organization's competencies related to the "Success for Leadership" model (draw a diagram)?

*Advice:*

- Focus on the content that is to be learned, rather than on broader lessons that participants may have learned. Just as teachers and professors will design classroom tests to measure students' knowledge of a particular subject, the learning survey should be designed to assess knowledge gain and will require working closely with a subject-matter expert.
- Although it is perfectly acceptable to measure depth of knowledge, you want to be careful that participants do not feel "tested" on areas that they should not be expected to have learned.

Change surveys. Surveys are useful in assessing whether change has occurred as a result of a development initiative. They are typically used to measure changes in attitudes or behaviors specific to the initiative in question. A well-developed set of survey questions on change should be based on what is already known about the impact of the initiative or the objectives of the initiative. They should also ensure that the response scale used in the change survey facilitates the measurement of change.

Using surveys to assess change is most effective when the focus of the evaluation is on behavioral changes as measured by primarily quantitative data. Administering a survey to assess change at different points in time has different purposes. For example, using a survey before and after an initiative allows the evaluator to identify behavioral shifts that have taken place as a result of the initiative. However, it is not always realistic to do a pre-initiative survey, and response-shift bias (see the section below) is a potential concern.

Valid, reliable survey questions on changes in leadership behaviors can be time-consuming to develop, but they can be relatively inexpensive to administer. Using a survey to assess change has some clear advantages:

- It provides the opportunity to capture responses from a large sample of people.
- It assures anonymity or confidentiality of responses.
- It has the ability to reach geographically dispersed respondents.
- It allows respondents to respond on their own time.
- It requires that all respondents answer the same set of questions.

On the minus side, this approach doesn't allow for changes to or clarification of questions, as is the case with interviews and focus groups.

Intuition can be misleading when developing a survey. Even seemingly simple choices, such as what response options to use, can have an unintended impact on results. If you plan to develop your own survey and do not have training in survey development, it is wise to seek advice from measurement or psychometric publications or from measurement professionals. Exhibit 3.5 contains examples of formats you should consider using when creating change surveys.

## Exhibit 3.5 – Examples of Change-Survey Formats

These examples show three ways to determine the changes that have occurred as a result of a leadership-development program. We use the same outcomes in each example. Most surveys of this type will include all of the major outcomes expected from the leadership-development initiative. Any of these change-survey formats can be used with participants, and with some tailoring they can also be administered to direct reports, peers, or managers of participants to gather multiple perspectives.

### Example 1:

This format requires one rating of change for each intended outcome. It provides only an "amount of improvement" rating as reported by the participant typically several months after the completion of a leadership-development experience. We don't usually see a need to include response options that reflect skills getting worse, but we do include the option for no change.

Using the rating scale provided below, please indicate the extent to which you have changed in the indicated areas as a result of this leadership-development initiative:

| | Not at All (1) | To a Little Extent (2) | To Some Extent (3) | To a Great Extent (4) | To a Very Great Extent (5) |
|---|---|---|---|---|---|
| I communicate better in difficult conversations. | ❍ | ❍ | ❍ | ❍ | ❍ |
| I am better able to encourage direct and open discussions about important issues. | ❍ | ❍ | ❍ | ❍ | ❍ |
| I am better at using active listening skills in conversations with others. | ❍ | ❍ | ❍ | ❍ | ❍ |
| I am better at adapting to different interpersonal needs for communication. | ❍ | ❍ | ❍ | ❍ | ❍ |

[And so on, until all objectives have been addressed.]

## Exhibit 3.5 – Examples of Change-Survey Formats (continued)

### Example 2:

This example uses a "Retrospective Before–Now" rating format. For this type of change measure, two ratings are collected from the participant for each intended outcome. This type of format provides a "current effectiveness" rating and allows for an "amount of improvement" rating (by subtracting the "Before" scores from the "Now" scores").

Using the rating scale provided, rate the following. Please provide ratings about the extent to which you (or the participant) exhibited the indicated behavior "Before" participating in the leadership-development initiative and your (or his/her) behavior "Now," after participating in the leadership-development initiative.

1 = Not at all
2 = To a minimal extent
3 = To a small extent
4 = To some extent
5 = To a moderate extent
6 = To a considerable extent
7 = To a large extent
8 = To a very great extent
9 = Completely

| Before the Initiative | Behaviors | Now |
|---|---|---|
| 1 2 3 4 5 6 7 8 9 | Communicate effectively in difficult conversations. | 1 2 3 4 5 6 7 8 9 |
| 1 2 3 4 5 6 7 8 9 | Encourage direct and open discussions about important issues. | 1 2 3 4 5 6 7 8 9 |
| 1 2 3 4 5 6 7 8 9 | Use active listening skills in conversations with others. | 1 2 3 4 5 6 7 8 9 |
| 1 2 3 4 5 6 7 8 9 | Adapt to different interpersonal needs for communication. | 1 2 3 4 5 6 7 8 9 |

## Exhibit 3.5 – Examples of Change-Survey Formats (continued)

### Example 3:

This example asks participants to rate the improvements they made as well as their current skill level. Unlike Example 2, it does not ask for past and current ratings on the same skill and is therefore less dependent on the participant being able to specifically rate his or her performance from several months prior to completing the survey. It can also be helpful to ask participants to describe changes they have made in their own words as seen in the final question in this example.

Use the rating scale provided to rate your performance on the following behaviors and improvement made on each behavior since participating in the leadership-development initiative.

| Behaviors | Current Effectiveness | | | | | Improvement | | | | |
|---|---|---|---|---|---|---|---|---|---|---|
| | None | | Moderate | | Great | None | | Moderate | | Great |
| Communicate effectively in difficult conversations. | 1 | 2 | 3 | 4 | 5 | 1 | 2 | 3 | 4 | 5 |
| Encourage direct and open discussions about important issues. | 1 | 2 | 3 | 4 | 5 | 1 | 2 | 3 | 4 | 5 |
| Use active listening skills in conversations with others. | 1 | 2 | 3 | 4 | 5 | 1 | 2 | 3 | 4 | 5 |
| Adapt to different interpersonal needs for communication. | 1 | 2 | 3 | 4 | 5 | 1 | 2 | 3 | 4 | 5 |

Please give an example of a significant change you have made as a result of participating in the program.

_______________________________________________

_______________________________________________

*Advice:*

- Determine what type of change you are looking for or expecting to find and then use the most appropriate types of questions to collect the data.
- Determine the most appropriate timing to measure the change you are looking for—some types of change can be assessed soon after an initiative ends, while others may take up to a year to become measurable.
- Ensure that you report the results in the way appropriate to the data collected. Depending on the type of questions and response format used, data may be reported as frequencies, means, difference scores, or in some other way. Providing the most information and meaning possible from whatever data are collected is critical to being able to communicate the changes that have been made.
- Consider including at least a few open-ended questions to capture examples of changes made and factors that help or hinder change, if you have the resources for analyzing qualitative responses for key themes.

## The Measurement of Change: Methods and Issues

Although individuals can sometimes agree that a situation or an individual has or has not changed, they are much less likely to agree on how much change has occurred and whether the change represents an improvement. How to best measure change remains a hotly debated topic. Below, we list some of the issues you might encounter when measuring change.

**Response-shift bias.** Bias occurs when individuals use a different definition of effectiveness than they used before the initiative or they have higher expectations for their performance. For example, a leader might rate themselves as a good leader before an initiative but then rate themselves the same or even lower after the initiative because they understand "good leadership" in a different way, or because after spending time with remarkable leaders, they see their performance in a different light.

**Demand characteristics and social desirability.** These are research terms, both related to the tendency of respondents to provide data indicating that the expected or desired changes have occurred, even if they have not. The respondents may not even be aware they are doing it, and the effect is difficult to avoid in retrospective measures.

Evaluators who use multi-rater, or 360-degree, surveys to measure how a leadership-development initiative has changed individual performance or behavior often use one of the following methods: pre- and post-initiative assessments, retrospective pretest and posttest assessments, and degree-of-change ratings.

**Pre- and post-initiative assessments.** In this approach the same assessment is administered before and after the leadership-development initiative. This technique is best suited for situations in which what you want to measure is very specific and concrete (easily observable). Although seemingly straightforward, changes in the organization (restructuring, layoffs, or new compensation systems, to name a few) and differences in the types and intensity of training can make the data difficult or impossible to interpret because too many factors might be related to the changes observed. Many leadership-development initiatives use 360-degree instruments to provide feedback to participants. To measure change, some organizations may want to use the same 360-degree instrument after the initiative. However, this approach can have some challenges. For example, if different raters are used, there may be changes in scores simply because different raters are providing information. Scores on scales, and particularly on questions, can fluctuate even though a person's "true" score remains the same because of things like a person's mood, what was happening when they completed the assessment, and so on. Comparing scores (question by question or scale by scale) to measure change over time or to measure the impact of an initiative or other leadership-development experience may provide misleading information. Offsetting some of these differences when comparing scores is difficult but can be done; for instance, having randomly assigned control and treatment groups or large numbers of participants can help in improving the likelihood that differences can be attributed to the program participation.

Another example is that organizational culture or climate (for instance, engagement surveys) are sometimes administered before and after a leadership-development initiative. Examples include measuring whether employees' perceptions of managers or senior leaders are changing as a result of the initiative or if the leaders themselves and the groups they lead are feeling more empowered and engaged as a result of the investment in their development. Again, there are limitations to this approach. For instance, just because there is movement on the assessment one way or another does not alone tell us anything about how or why the changes occurred.

**Retrospective pretest and posttest assessments.** Retrospective pretest and posttest assessments require two ratings like the pre- and post-initiative assessments. However, items are posed that require the two ratings (for pre-participation and post-participation) at the same time after participants have completed the initiative. One rating usually focuses on describing an individual participant before the intervention. The second rating assesses the person's skills and behaviors at the time the survey is completed after the intervention. The participants, their bosses, and other stakeholders can be involved in the rating process and it can help assuage some of the limitations of having two separate time periods to complete the ratings mentioned with the previously discussed pre- and post-initiative assessments.

There are also limitations in using retrospective assessments. Although some literature suggests that inflationary biases in retrospective assessments are nearly unavoidable, there are strategies that can be employed that help offset these limitations and make it a stronger design. If using this approach, you must be sure that your questions are behaviorally based and are very specific in outlining the behavior that is expected to change because of the initiative. Similar considerations of timing and intensity of training need to be made to try to ensure that change is possible because of the program. In other words, collecting this type of information with an established, more intensive program is more appropriate than for a short, new pilot program, as the newer program might have shifting objectives because it is a pilot session where more formative, improvement feedback is especially appropriate.

**Degree-of-change ratings.** Another method for measuring change is to ask individuals to rate the degree of change using a response scale. For example, raters could select from a five-point scale ranging from "no change" to "great change." Research has indicated that there seems to be more agreement across rater groups (peers, direct reports, and bosses, for example) as to the amount of change when all groups are rating change directly, as compared with evaluations that measure change using pre- and posttest ratings (Peterson, 1993).

Organizational or social-network survey. A network in its most basic sense is a set of nodes and the ties that connect them. Nodes can be people, groups, or organizations, and the ties that connect them can represent influence, collaboration, partnership agreements, or any number of other relationships of interest. Building or increasing the effectiveness of networks is often implicitly and explicitly an outcome of leadership solutions. As such, network surveys and analysis can be valuable in evaluation of initiatives when used under the right conditions.

Network analysis is most useful when the leadership-development initiative is expected to result in observable changes to a network. Expected outcomes should be clearly defined, and there should be solid logic behind why a particular initiative should lead to the outcomes. Further, they should be specific. For instance "changes in our organizational network" is vague; "increase in collaboration on projects between Division A and Division B within one year" is specific and actionable. The expected changes should be at the level of the group/team/organization rather than the individual. Finally, the outcomes should also be connected to a broader goal or organizational strategy.

Common examples of outcomes where network analysis could be useful:

- To increase intra- or intergroup connectivity/collaboration
- To spark strategic networks to address specific initiatives within or beyond their organization
- To integrate certain groups of individuals more fully into the network (for instance, onboarding, integrating minority groups)
- To increase the involvement of a wider range of organizational members in leadership

Below is an example of a network survey that participants might be asked to fill out before a leadership-development initiative.

## Exhibit 3.6 – Example of a Network Survey

Prior to participating in the Leadership Development Program, please respond to this survey. You will also be asked to respond to a similar survey in 6 months. The data will be used to understand how relationships among people in the Leadership Development Program change over time. Network maps like the one created below will be provided by all participants and shared as part of the program to help the group understand its current connectivity and co-develop ways to improve.

Below is a list of participants and the departments they represent. Please read over the list and choose the individuals with whom you have any level of familiarity. Be sure to choose anyone that you may know, even if you have heard of an individual only by name. You will be able to tell us more about the nature of your relationship with these individuals in the following questions.

__ John Costello, Marketing
__ Laura Fernandez, Sales
__ Samir Doshi, Research
__ Constantine Spencer, Sales

Please indicate your level of familiarity with each of the participants you choose.

| | I have heard of but not met this person | I have met this person but do not know him/her well | I know this person reasonably well | I know this person very well |
|---|---|---|---|---|
| John Costello, Marketing | | | | |
| Samir Doshi, Research | | | | |

**Exhibit 3.6 – Example of a Network Survey** (continued)

If you have collaborated on a work-related project within the past year with any of the following people, please describe how.

By collaboration, we mean you have exchanged information or discussed ideas, shared resources (for example, websites, contacts, funding opportunities), or participated in joint implementation of an activity related to the mission of your organization (as distinguished from sharing advice or encouragement for individual concerns).

Select all options that apply. If you have not collaborated with an individual listed, please leave the response blank.

| | Exchanged information or discussed ideas | Shared resources | Jointly implemented an activity |
|---|---|---|---|
| John Costello, Marketing | | | |
| Samir Doshi, Research | | | |

*Advice:*

- Discuss expected outcomes and expectations with stakeholders to identify what kind of network data will be most useful. For instance, more connections do not necessarily mean a better network.
- Ensure timing of administration makes sense given the intervention and when outcomes would be expected. Discuss short- versus long-term effects; could short-term "wins" actually result in long-term problems?
- Set clear expectations about data presentation and confidentiality. Network data cannot be collected anonymously. The level of confidentiality needs to be carefully discussed and communicated to participants. When planning how to share results, consider whether any names will be displayed or whether the individuals in any network positions will be identified.
- Network analysis should be part of a larger evaluation approach. Additional qualitative data should be collected to understand the changes that are observed and how they are connected to the broader outcomes.
- Ensure a high level of participation. A high response rate is required for network analysis. The general rule is that an 80% response rate (Marsden, 1990) is needed to have confidence that an adequate representation of the network has been captured. One option is to embed participation in network analysis into the development initiative so that it is part of the requirements for participation.
- Ensure there is a clearly defined group/team to focus on (intact group). The most straightforward case is to examine the same bounded network over time. For example, administering

the survey to the same group of people, division, cohort, and so on at multiple points in time.

- Recognize that collecting and sharing network data (time 1) *is* part of an intervention; consider what implications that has for the evaluation.

Network analysis is not appropriate for every evaluation design. It requires a unique skill set, special software, and can be very labor-intensive. There are multiple resources available to better understand how network analysis has been or could be used in evaluation of leadership-development initiatives: for instance, how to frame the evaluation questions (Hoppe & Reinelt, 2010), what effective networks look like (Krebs & Holley, 2006), how network analysis has been used in evaluation of leadership-development programs (Fredericks & Carman, 2013), and understanding social networks' role in leadership (Cullen, Palus, & Appaneal, 2013).

**Interviews.** Interview questions are typically open-ended, provide qualitative data, and can be asked either face-to-face, by videoconference, or by telephone. You can conduct interviews to determine the level of knowledge, skills, and attitudes gained from an individual's experience with a development initiative. You can also use interviews to assess perceptions of the initiative from a stakeholder's perspective. In addition, you can obtain examples of how behavior has changed or how what was learned has been applied and what changes resulted. If resources don't allow time for one-on-one interviews, you can adapt the interview format to an open-ended questionnaire that you can mail or e-mail to participants.

Interviews are most effective when you want qualitative information to fulfill multiple purposes. Such purposes include:

- assisting in identifying training and learning needs, improving an initiative's design, or gathering expectations for applying lessons from the development initiative (interviews would take place before the initiative);
- determining participants' reactions, experiences, and satisfaction with the initiative (interviews would take place during a longer-term initiative);
- determining participants' reactions, learning, and intentions to apply their learning (interviews would take place during an initiative or after it had ended);
- developing surveys, focus-group interview questions, or the focus of an observation (interviews could take place at any point relative to an initiative, depending on the outcomes desired); and
- helping to interpret survey results (interviews can be used to enhance your understanding and insights gained from surveys).

Interviews have several advantages and disadvantages. One advantage is that they allow the evaluator to probe for clarification and deeper complexity, which results in richer data. And, they provide time for participants and stakeholders to reflect, which can be developmental in itself. A significant disadvantage is that interviews can be more costly than other methods. If the interviews are conducted in person, for example, travel costs add to the total price of the evaluation. Interviews can also take more of the evaluator's time, both in terms of conducting the interviews and analyzing the qualitative data. Exhibit 3.7 below contains several examples of interview protocols that could be employed.

***Advice:***

- Consider conducting interviews by Skype or other electronic collaboration tools; these reduce travel costs and allow evaluators to conduct more interviews in a shorter amount of time. With the ability to use video, it is easier than it used to be to build rapport and to "read" nonverbal communication despite not being in a room together. If "sensitive" information is sought in the interview, if building trust is a concern, or if the organization's culture isn't highly supportive of virtual conversations, it may be worth the extra expense of conducting face-to-face interviews to ensure higher quality data are provided.
- When scheduling interviews, let interviewees know approximately how long the interview will take and, if at all possible, provide them with the questions in advance.
- If multiple people will be conducting interviews, you may want to review the protocol together to be sure everyone understands what kind of follow-up questions might be needed so that consistent data are collected.
- If the evaluator conducts the interviews (as opposed to the organization's talent department, for example), acceptance and endorsement for the evaluation can increase, because participants and stakeholders often view the evaluator as an objective party.

## Exhibit 3.7 – Examples of Interview Questions

### *Participant Interview Protocol: Rating Questions*

The first three questions I am going to ask you are rating questions. For each question, please respond using a 5-point scale, with 1 being "not at all" and 5 being "to a great extent."

1. To what extent have you applied the tools, frameworks, and models you learned during the program in your work?

2. To what extent did the program help you develop leadership skills that resulted in you being more effective as a leader?

    a. Is there any particular leadership skill at which you are more effective?

    b. How did the program help with that?

3. To what extent did the program help you develop or improve collaborative relationships with other leaders in your organization?

### *Participant Interview Protocol: Semi-Structured Interview Questions*

Now we will move into the main interview questions. Feel free to elaborate as much as you would like and to provide any specific examples that you think would be helpful.

1. What was the most valuable part of the program for you?

2. Now, reflecting back on the entire program experience, what is the biggest change you made as a result of the program?

    a. What was the impact of that change for you personally?

    b. What was the impact of that change in the part of the organization you lead?

    c. Why was this important (what value was created)?

    d. What aspects of the program helped you make this change? (Probe to get details.)

    e. What factors contributed to your success or to this success? [contextual factors]

3. What other significant changes have you made (revisit subquestions a. through e.)?

## Exhibit 3.7 – Examples of Interview Questions (continued)

4. Have you had any changes in your career since participating in the program (be sure to document career changes, for instance, promotion, lateral move)?

5. Is there anything that could have been different about the program that might have increased the impact for you?

6. Is there anything else you would like to tell me about your experience with the program or the impact of the program before we conclude this interview?

***Evaluation of a Program: Questions for Interviews with Senior Executives***

1. What kinds of leadership/management challenges were your managers aiming to address through this program? Probe: What did you see as the overall goal of the initiative? What were you hoping the managers would get out of it? What were you hoping your organization would get out of it?

2. What have you observed regarding the impact of this program on the managers who report to you and their teams? Specifically, did you see improvements in the leadership challenges they were facing (mentioned above)?

3. What have been the most significant changes you have observed in the managers who participated in this program? Probe (if you don't get specific examples): Can you give some concrete examples of the kinds of changes you have observed? (Make sure interviewee is okay with this example being shared in a group report. Again, focus on changes or improvements related to leadership/management challenges that this person hoped the program would help address with the participants.)

4. What, if any, impact have you observed on the organization as a result of this program?

5. What, if any, barriers do you see the managers facing in their ability to make changes in their leadership effectiveness after participating in the program?

6. In what areas do you think the managers need additional development to become more effective leaders?

7. Is there anything else that you feel is important to share about the impact of this program?

- Gather specific stories and examples of how the initiative impacted participants and stakeholders.
- If the data are confidential you will need to remove any names or titles used in the interviews. You may also need to remove specific examples used in the interviews if the examples make it clear who provided them.
- Include adequate time for analysis of the data. It will be most helpful if you can identify cross-cutting themes to provide useful insights about the implementation of the initiative, its impact, and the context in which the development and application of learning is taking place.
- It can be helpful to report how many people mentioned similar themes. For instance, "phone coaching was mentioned by 15 interviewees as a critical and beneficial aspect of their leadership-development experience, while 5 people did not think phone coaching was helpful at all."

## Success Case Method

The Success Case Method is an approach developed by Robert Brinkerhoff in which the individuals or groups who achieved the most and the least successful business outcomes are identified through a survey and then interviewed in more depth to determine what contributed to and what got in the way of success. The most and least successful cases can be identified by a survey or interviews about people or groups who successfully applied what they learned in the initiative. The approach can be a cost-effective and relatively quick way to get a sense of what is working well and what isn't. The following steps are part of using the Success Case Method:

- Create an initiative impact model that defines success.
- Identify the most and least successful cases (this is typically done using a survey, but not always).
- Interview the selected individuals to capture what from the initiative was applied, what contributed to and what got in the way of successful application, and the related business impact.
- Interpret and share information.

Focus Groups. You can use a focus group to interview multiple people at one time. Focus groups usually include about six to ten people. The primary purpose of this method is to obtain qualitative information from a group of individuals (or a team) that has had a similar experience (participation in a training program, for example). There are several excellent resources for evaluators considering using focus groups (Greenbaum, 1999; Morgan, 1993; Morgan & Krueger, 1997).

Evaluations usually make use of multiple focus groups and use a well-designed guide to focus the discussion. Focus groups should be carried out in a way that allows participants to feel safe disclosing information about their attitudes and perceptions about the initiative being evaluated. Focus groups can take place face-to-face, over the phone, or online. Online focus groups can be conducted synchronously or asynchronously. Conducting an asynchronous online focus group can be a good choice when it is not possible to gather a group together because of conflicting schedules or because people are not co-located and travel is not an option. A side benefit of asynchronous online focus groups is that the conversation is automatically documented; a drawback is that facilitating the group conversation can be difficult and the online discussion might not be as engaging for participants.

There are several ways you can use focus groups in your evaluation. Before an initiative begins, you can use focus groups to identify training or learning needs, to determine an initiative's design, or to assess expectations of how participants will apply what they learn. During an initiative (assuming the initiative takes place over several days, weeks, or months), you can use a focus group to determine participants' reactions to and experiences and satisfaction with the development initiative. After the initiative ends, you can use this evaluation method to determine participants' reactions, what they've learned,

## Online Focus Groups

Advances in the use of online tools to facilitate and conduct online focus groups are increasingly being discussed in the evaluation field and literature. Online focus groups are sometimes more likely to promote more open disclosure of positive and negative feedback, to encourage wider participation because one person does not dominate the conversation, and to provide a digital record of the exchange. However, challenges of online focus groups include the increased difficulty in troubleshooting the technology as it is happening and abbreviated statements are included rather than full quotes.

Advice for using online focus groups:

- Try to use the platform that the participants typically use in their business.
- Use text as well as voice discussions to allow participants the freedom to answer with their preferred methods.
- Decide whether you want to send the focus group questions in advance of the focus group so respondents can consider their answers beforehand or if you want more spontaneous answers.
- Think about ways to anonymize participants (a general dial-in number, for instance) if possible.
- Have someone in charge of troubleshooting technology with the participants, with no other responsibility, before and during the online focus group.
- Pose one question at a time if you are doing a synchronous online group. Reading the question aloud as well as having a text prompt will give participants a reminder of the question posed.

how they intend to apply their new skills and knowledge, and the relative successes or challenges they've had in doing so. Focus groups are also effective when it's necessary to assess reactions, learning, and intentions of a team rather than individual participants. See Exhibits 3.8 and 3.9 for examples.

Some evaluators use focus groups to develop survey questions or to further interpret survey results. Another useful aspect of them is that they allow participants to process their experiences together, which can help them build support networks to further aid in their development. Focus groups can be used to collect data from initiative designers, staff, and client contacts as well.

The focus-group data-collection method has several advantages. Because it captures the collective experience of individuals, interaction among participants tends to increase the number and quality of responses. It provides a forum for teams to create additional impact and meaning related to their developmental experience. It lets the interviewer probe for clarification, explanations, and examples. Participants generally enjoy taking part, resulting in high response rates. This method is relatively inexpensive and makes good use of time in that it allows evaluators to collect data quickly from a large group of people.

The focus-group method also has some limitations. A skilled interviewer is required to ensure that the data collected are of high quality. The interviewer has less control in a group interview than in an individual interview and so needs to have the skills and ability to keep the group on track. Data collected from a focus group may be difficult to capture and organize. Groups vary widely—some groups may develop a collective energy and provide extensive data, while others may lack energy and provide only superficial data.

## Exhibit 3.8 – Example of a Focus Group

### Leadership Program Pilot: Focus-Group Moderator's Guide

*Instructions for participants.* The purpose of this focus group is to gain an understanding of what your experience was like participating in this leadership-development initiative. There are no right or wrong answers. What you share with us will help us understand the impact that participating in this program has had on you and on the organization. It will also help improve the program for the future. Please be honest and open about your experience. We will be recording this conversation and taking notes; however, we will keep your responses confidential. We are looking for themes across all of the participants. We will not share your individual responses with anyone, including anyone at this organization. We may want to quote something you have said, but we will only indicate that it was said by a participant or will follow up with you for permission to use your name.

*Warm up.* Please tell me your name and which part of the initiative was most memorable for you.

*Preparation phase.* Let's talk about your experience in more detail. First, I'd like for you to think about the preparation phase: everything that happened before the three-day session began.

- How well did program staff set your expectations for the assignments that you completed prior to the session?
- Is there anything else we should know about regarding the preparation phase before coming to this session?

*Program phase.* Now I want to talk about everything that happened while you were attending the session this week.

- Which components of the session content were most useful to you? Were there any components that were not useful? [If not mentioned, probe for the following: nonverbal communication, conflict, influence, one-on-one coaching session.]
- Were there any times throughout the session when you felt that a certain module, activity, or example wasn't relevant to your job or to how things work at this organization? What examples do you have?
- Thinking about the assessments you used during the initiative, which ones stand out in your mind, and which were most valuable? [If not mentioned, probe for the following: FIRO-B, 360.)
- How well did the trainers and coaches do in helping you understand your assessment results and how to apply them?

*(continued)*

**Exhibit 3.8 – Example of a Focus Group** (continued)

You've all been part of the leadership series for several months now and have participated in two other face-to-face sessions as part of the initiative. How did you think this week's session fit with the other parts of the initiative?

- Did it complement and add to what you've already been working on?
- What did you think about the interactive nature of the initiative compared to others you have attended? Too much/about right/not enough?

Let's talk about ways that you were able to tie together or integrate what you learned this week. How useful was:

- Working on one key leadership challenge?
- Creating the connection maps?
- Goal setting?
- Connecting with your learning group?

***Post-program phase.*** Okay, now let's talk about what will happen beginning next week.

- How equipped do you feel to make some changes you've identified?
- Do you have any concerns about the six follow-up coaching calls that you will have?
- What tools or information can program staff provide to help you?
- What skills would you like to develop next? What topics should we offer?

***Recommendations and improvements.*** Please consider the following:

- Would you recommend this type of program to a colleague? Why or why not?
- What is the one thing that you would make sure that program staff changes or improves about this program?
- What is the one thing we should keep or definitely *not* change?

## Exhibit 3.9 – Focus Group: Several Months After the Initiative

- Since the cohort last met, what can you add to your "story" of the impact of your participation in the Leadership Development Program on:
    - Your own leadership effectiveness?
    - The effectiveness of the teams you lead?
    - The effectiveness of your organization?
- What outcomes has your action-learning project delivered to date? What, if any, additional outcomes do you anticipate delivering?
- How effective was your action-learning project from a learning perspective?
- What "grade" (A, B, C, D, or F) would you give to the Leadership Development Program as a whole, if it were subjected to a report card? Why?
- Has being a member of the Leadership Development Program increased the visibility of participants, including being considered for open positions? Can you provide an example?
- What has been the effect of the Leadership Development Program on your commitment to your organization? Are you more committed or less committed, or is your commitment about the same as compared to your commitment to your organization before you participated in the Leadership Development Program?
- As you look back over this experience, how would you describe the support you've had to participate?
- What has been missing, in terms of support you wish you'd had to participate?
- How would you evaluate the success of the Leadership Development Program? Specifically, how was it as a mechanism for:
    - Individual development?
    - Networking/building relationships?
    - Creating an impact on the organization?
- What additional insights would you like to share about the Leadership Development Program?

*Advice:*

- Be sure you are ready to facilitate a focus group before beginning. Focus groups are more than a process of asking questions—group facilitation is extremely important to keep the focus on the questions at hand versus detouring into a tangential conversation.
- Be aware of whether all members of the focus group are sharing their perspective—do not let a few voices dominate, but be sensitive to power differences that may prevent a person from feeling his or her perspective can be safely voiced.
- Know the dynamics of the group—know whether you will need to continually probe for details or whether group members will openly communicate their perspectives.
- Do not voice your opinion during the focus group—remain in the evaluator role, even though you may want to answer participants' questions about your stance.
- When focus groups are used to get a quick response at the end of an initiative, make sure you allow time to analyze the data and generate a report or presentation quickly after the focus group takes place.
- Aggregate the data rather than reporting who said what. However, if examples are given that connect to a specific individual and if those examples will be particularly powerful for the evaluation report, get permission from the participant(s) to use those examples before including them in reports.

**Archival documents and data.** Documents and records are written statements and other materials that attest to an event or provide an accounting of some activity. Evaluators who use documents typically wish to make inferences about the values, sentiments, intentions, or beliefs of the sources or authors.

Documents include letters, journals, logs, position papers, notes, speeches, newspaper articles and editorials, annual reports, newsletters, case studies, evaluation or consultants' reports, and photographs. Records are typically used to keep track of events or transactions. They might include expenditure records, expense-account vouchers, financial information, performance records, student or participant achievement or performance test records, state or federal regulatory records, attendance records, competency or attitude score records, and electronic-mail records.

This method can be effective in understanding the history or background of an initiative or situation; in tracking the number of times that something has occurred; in helping develop survey or interview questions or areas on which to focus an observation; in identifying patterns of participation, interest in, or attitudes toward an initiative; and in better understanding an issue that people are unable or unwilling to talk about.

Document analysis has several advantages as a method of data collection. Documents and records are often plentiful (stored usually in the organization's archives) and inexpensive to collect. Data from documents and records may provide useful chronological detail (possibly more accurately than a chronology built from interviews). The data gathered from documents and records are less subject to an evaluator's bias than data from interviews and observation. When used with other methods, documents and records provide a contextual richness for interpreting other data collected during the evaluation.

There are also some limitations. For example, samples of documents or records may not be representative (notes from some meetings may exist but not from others). Personal documents may reflect a person's bias. Deliberate deception or manipulation of information is possible if a document's writer had a desire to express a certain viewpoint. Also, records may contain incomplete or out-of-date information.

***Advice:***

- In many evaluation situations, the amount of archival data that could possibly be collected is almost endless. Be sure that you only collect what is needed and what is realistic to report.
- If at all possible, make good use of archival data early in an evaluation process to help you create other methods of data collection to be used subsequently.
- When leadership-development initiatives include projects, action-learning experiences, or other forms of action that participants are expected to report upon, the presentations and reports from those projects are excellent documents to include in your evaluation because they address actions and outcomes directly tied to the initiative itself.
- Use examples from the archival data when possible, paying attention to gaining permission before reporting anything that might be confidential.
- If it is important to make samples available to key stakeholders who receive your report, think about posting the samples in an electronic format accessible to recipients.

**Workplace statistics.** Workplace statistics include information that organizations gather such as promotions, absenteeism, retention, customer satisfaction, sales revenue, time-to-launch, employee engagement, etc. Evaluators can obtain this information from the organization and analyze it in relation to the leadership-development initiative and its objectives. Before requesting and using statistics in an evaluation project, carefully determine which statistics are likely to change as a result of an individual's, team's, or group's participation in the initiative.

Using these types of metrics to understand the impact of a leadership-development initiative is useful when the initiative is designed to meet specific organizational outcomes. For example, when participants are expected (as part of their action plan based on their development experience) to work differently with at-risk employees to prevent situations that might lead to grievances, it is appropriate and useful to examine the change in frequency and severity of grievances that employees file. When the head of a health clinic, as a result of participating in leadership development, sets goals related to encouraging better patient relations, it would be useful to examine patient satisfaction data as well as wait times and patient return visits.

Statistics aren't useful if there aren't links between the statistics, the expected organizational outcomes, and the development initiative. (Refer to Chapter Two to assess whether this method is an appropriate evaluation approach for your situation.) When analyzing the connection between workplace metrics and the leadership-development initiative is not feasible, a survey can capture perceptions of business impact of the initiative. See below for a survey example.

## Exhibit 3.10 – Example of Workplace-Statistics Survey

The following survey was developed as a means of assessing self-reported and manager-reported evidence of return on investment resulting from a leadership-development initiative.

**Business Outcomes**

Please provide a numeric rating for each of the outcomes listed below or indicate NR if the outcome is not relevant to your situation.

My own development and improved leadership effectiveness have contributed to organizational change as expressed below:

| | |
|---|---|
| 1 = Decreased dramatically | 4 = Increased |
| 2 = Decreased | 5 = Increased dramatically |
| 3 = Not changed | NR = Not relevant |

| | | | | | | |
|---|---|---|---|---|---|---|
| 1. Productivity within the group I lead has . . . | 1 | 2 | 3 | 4 | 5 | NR |
| 2. Profit within the group I lead has . . . | 1 | 2 | 3 | 4 | 5 | NR |
| 3. Level of trust and collaboration within the group I lead has . . . | 1 | 2 | 3 | 4 | 5 | NR |
| 4. Customer satisfaction with the group I lead has . . . | 1 | 2 | 3 | 4 | 5 | NR |
| 5. Customer loyalty to the group I lead has . . . | 1 | 2 | 3 | 4 | 5 | NR |
| 6. Employee job satisfaction among my subordinate group has . . . | 1 | 2 | 3 | 4 | 5 | NR |
| 7. Employee promotions among my subordinate group have . . . | 1 | 2 | 3 | 4 | 5 | NR |
| 8. The number of training programs attended by employees in my group has . . . | 1 | 2 | 3 | 4 | 5 | NR |
| 9. Employee job effectiveness among my subordinate group has . . . | 1 | 2 | 3 | 4 | 5 | NR |

**Exhibit 3.10 – Example of Workplace-Statistics Survey (continued)**

|  | | | | | | |
|---|---|---|---|---|---|---|
| 10. Innovation within the group I lead has . . . | 1 | 2 | 3 | 4 | 5 | NR |
| 11. Implementation of new ideas within the group I lead has . . . | 1 | 2 | 3 | 4 | 5 | NR |
| 12. Successful completion of projects within the group I lead has . . . | 1 | 2 | 3 | 4 | 5 | NR |
| 13. New products and services developed within the group I lead have . . . | 1 | 2 | 3 | 4 | 5 | NR |
| 14. Absenteeism among my subordinate group has . . . | 1 | 2 | 3 | 4 | 5 | NR |
| 15. Tardiness among my subordinate group has . . . | 1 | 2 | 3 | 4 | 5 | NR |
| 16. Employee turnover among my subordinate group has . . . | 1 | 2 | 3 | 4 | 5 | NR |
| 17. Requests for employee transfers among my subordinate group have . . . | 1 | 2 | 3 | 4 | 5 | NR |

Provide quantitative evidence for the two areas (above) that have shown the most impact (for example, the percent of increased employee promotions among your subordinate group or money saved because of a particular change you've implemented).

***Advice:***

- The richness of statistics is vast, if the data represent direct or indirect outcomes of the leadership-development initiative. It is well worth your time to work with stakeholders long enough to identify critical and realistic links.
- Ensure that stakeholders understand what will be part of the evaluation and their relationship to the initiative so that (a) data are provided to you and (b) stakeholders support your use of the data.
- Design the evaluation plan so that you are collecting data that can represent trends for a period of time that makes sense, relative to the changes you anticipate.
- Understand any limitations on the reporting of statistics before you report them. When data represent human resources or confidential issues, you need to understand any agreements under which they were collected before you share them.

## Measuring Return on Investment (ROI)

Although *return on investment* is a phrase that most often refers to financial implications, it can also describe the broader impact of individual and team-development initiatives on an organization. Several methods are available to evaluate such impact. Determining which is the most appropriate for a particular evaluation depends on the type of impact expected (see, for example, Chapter Five in Hannum, Martineau, & Reinelt, 2007). To identify the appropriate measure at the organizational level, some useful questions to ask include the following:

- What changes are expected as a result of the initiative?
- Why are these changes expected? (In other words, what is the connection between the objectives of the leadership-development experience and these changes?)
- When can stakeholders in the organization or in the community expect to see changes?
- Who will be able to note and report on these changes?
- How can data about these changes be obtained?

True measures of ROI include data such as the costs of facilities, trainers, materials, and the time participants spend in training and away from their jobs. ROI formulas also include the financial benefits of training, such as cost savings, new revenue, and calculations of the value of perceived job improvement (Phillips, Phillips, & Ray, 2012). The financial costs and benefits of some leadership-development outcomes can be difficult and expensive to measure and quantify. For example, what is the value of different groups sharing information more effectively with one another? A critical step in creating accurate ROI formulas is to establish a connection between outcomes and intervention and isolating and measuring the effects of development. For example, is the increase in product sales a result of the leadership-development initiative or the new marketing campaign that was launched?

Although ROI formulas work well for skills-based training and many organizations apply them to leadership development, there are challenges to using this method. It doesn't provide data related to the quality of improvement. For example, an ROI of 300% is impressive, but without data showing where the improvement has been made, it's not possible to fully measure the impact of that improvement. Additionally, given the time and effort required to conduct a thorough ROI evaluation, it is not an approach that can widely be applied. The experts on ROI methodology recommend this approach for 5 to 10% of training programs.

Observation. Observation involves watching a set of activities, the people who are participating in those activities, and the environment in which the activities take place. Observations can produce qualitative data in the form of field notes or quantitative data if observers note their information as ratings, rankings, or frequencies. Exhibit 3.11 below contains examples of data obtained from behavioral observations.

There are several effective uses for observation. Before the initiative begins, it can determine participants' baseline knowledge, skills or behaviors, and attitudes. During the initiative it can determine levels of interaction, engagement, skill development, and satisfaction with the initiative. Observations conducted between one week and three to six months after completion of the initiative can determine changes in knowledge, skills or behaviors, and attitudes. Observation is especially effective when it is used as one of several data-collection methods. Observations can be done in person, or using video recordings.

Compared with other evaluation methods, behavioral observation has several advantages. For example, data are collected where the activity is taking place, thus enhancing the data's validity; target activities are viewed within a context that may help interpret data collected from other methods; a trained observer might see things that others

**Exhibit 3.11 – Behavioral Observations**

Observations can focus on individual behaviors or the interactions between people. Describe behaviors that indicate that participants are accepting feedback from others.

- *Pat listened as Fred explained that her behaviors made him feel uncomfortable in the meeting.*
- *Pat thanked Fred for the feedback and told him how she would try to change those particular behaviors in the future.*
- *Pat asked Fred to continue to feel comfortable in sharing his feedback with her.*

Describe behaviors that indicate that participants are delivering feedback to others.

- *Pat told Mary that her presentation was well received by the client but needed to be tightened for the next presentation.*
- *Pat gave Mary suggestions for tightening her presentation.*
- *Pat made herself available to Mary for future questions.*

Describe behaviors that indicate that participants are working effectively across organizational boundaries.

- *Pat negotiated with the materials-development director regarding a new product.*
- *Pat and the materials-development director worked together to resolve the issue.*
- *Pat and the materials-development director together presented the solution to senior management.*

close to the initiative may miss; and the observation process can illuminate issues that interviewees are unwilling to talk about.

This evaluation method also has some major limitations. It requires a well-trained observer. Multiple observers may focus on different things, thus making analysis and synthesis more difficult. Also, participants may alter their behavior if they know they are being observed. Finally, behavioral observation can be disruptive to the work environment and can be expensive because of the time involved for data collection and data synthesis, especially if a large sample is required.

***Advice:***

- First and foremost, be sure that behavioral observation will provide the data you are seeking. Given the time investment, it is an expensive method to conduct and you want to be sure you are getting your value out of it. Because the targeted development of leadership is so often observable only through natural (rather than simulated) interactions with others, observers may sometimes interfere with what would otherwise occur.
- Be as unobtrusive as possible as an observer.
- Ensure that you have permission to observe—it is unethical to make observations without the permission of those being observed.
- Let the person or people being observed know that they are allowed to ask you to stop observing should a situation arise that is uncomfortable or confidential—especially if it is unrelated to changes expected from the leadership-development efforts.
- Ensure that you present the results in a confidential way—do not disclose the individual or group being observed when you provide examples of your observations.

- Present the observations in terms of themes, with examples and, if appropriate, frequencies to represent the number of times you observed a particular behavior of interest.

**Projective techniques/photovoice.** Photovoice, at its origins, is a community-based, participatory research method used to give a voice to marginalized populations (for instance, impoverished people, women, minorities) who traditionally have little voice in the community. Participants are trained to use video and photo images to capture their experiences and stories. The pictures can then be used to highlight their condition and to initiate change.

This approach primarily has been used as an advocacy tool. However, more recently it has also been adapted for use as an evaluation method. Participants are instructed to take pictures to reflect the impact and most significant changes from participating in a program or initiative. CCL has used photovoice with participants to capture the impact that participating in a leadership-development initiative has had on them. Using methods like photovoice, in addition to traditional approaches, can lead to a richer understanding of programs' outcomes.

## Using Story-Telling to Describe Change

The Most Significant Change (MSC) is a participatory evaluation technique developed by Rick Davies. The MSC process involves the collection and use of significant change stories (SC). The purpose of MSC is to focus more on the learning aspect of an initiative as opposed to accountability for results. Also, MSC includes the use of purposeful sampling, which requires a more-in-depth examination of cases and stories. The following steps are useful to the implementation of MSC:

- Start and raise interest through the use of champions and knowing the approach.
- Create and define domains of change.
- Create and define the reporting period.
- Collect SCs.
- Review and select the most significant stories within the organization.
- Provide stakeholders with feedback about the results.
- Verify the stories (if necessary).
- Quantification.
- Do meta monitoring and conduct secondary analysis.
- Review and revise the MSC process (Davies & Dart, 2005).

**Data storage and treatment.** Data collected as part of an evaluation often contain information that is private and confidential and the security and protection of these data is critical. Moreover, in the current context of cloud storage and data sharing, traditional ways of accounting for and protecting data have become outdated. Therefore, you will need to consider both traditional and new ways to protect the data.

Here are some things to keep in mind:

- Keep confidential data secure (a locked room and cabinet, a password-protected and encrypted electronic file, backed up on a shared or cloud-based drive, limited shared folder space with specific ending dates of access, partitioning data into pieces with multiple levels of access codes, and so on). If you are not certain about how private or confidential the data are, it is generally better to be overly cautious.
- Check the cloud providers that you are using. Pay attention to the terms and conditions of service and privacy policies. If you are using a service, you need to know who controls the information stored with the service. A few questions to consider include the following: What happens to the data when I save or delete a file? Is there a mirror document elsewhere? Who has access to this from the cloud company? What are the risks as a user if there is a loss of data or disruption in service? If there are mobile applications associated with the cloud storage, what happens to these if security is breached?

- You may want to keep a duplicate copy of data that are critical to an evaluation. To save space you may want to scan paper documents and keep them stored electronically.
- For confidential data, consider using a coding scheme (an identification number, for example) rather than the name of a person or group so if data are compromised, no one will be able to identify who provided the data.
- If you need to combine information from different sources, make sure you have an identifier for each data source that is common. For instance, use the same identification code for a person's interview and survey data. This approach also helps eliminate the need to gather basic information multiple times, because you can link information (it reduces redundancy and respondent frustration of providing the same information over and over).

Data analysis. Given the range of data sources we have included, providing detailed information about how to analyze each type of data isn't possible. There are also wonderful resources to help you analyze specific kinds of data. But we'd be remiss if we didn't offer you some guidance.

If possible, pull together all the data you will be working with into one platform and keep a back-up copy (just in case). Label your files and your variables with intuitive titles and review the data for errors before you begin analysis. For example, if the Women's Leadership Program has data from mainly male respondents, something probably isn't coded accurately. Or if knowing the interview location is important, then make sure you have it accurately labeled on all transcripts before you start working with data. Make sure the labels you use for variables and responses make sense. The numbers have no inherent meaning so you'll want to be sure you document what a response indicates. For example, if a "2" indicates that the respondent selected "female" as the gender with which they most identify, then be sure to document that in the data file itself or in a data map. If you combine data to create new variables, document what data you combined and how. You will also want to keep a log of how you went about analyzing your data in case there are questions about your approach later.

Assuming you have multiple sources of data, and we highly suggest that you do, you'll want to look across the different sources to see if the information seems to tell a consistent and reasonable story, or if data seem to conflict with each other; this process is referred to as data triangulation. For example, it is a red flag if program satisfaction ratings are high but interview data suggest high levels of frustration and dissatisfaction. As you analyze data, keep the context surrounding the data collection in mind and consider rival explanations. For example, if the program satisfaction data were gathered using paper forms by the trainers just after the social hour (where alcoholic beverages were served), then participants may not have been comfortable providing low ratings or may have been in such a good mood they would have rated almost anything highly—or if you only have data from 10% of participants, you may not have enough data or good enough data to say much with confidence.

If you get into data analysis and realize important information is missing or something essential to know doesn't make sense, it may not be too late to revise the evaluation plan to gather additional data for targeted needs. It is not a position you want to find yourself in, which is why planning is so important, but you may be able to get the resources and time needed if you explain the situation. Before moving into interpretation and communication of findings you want to be sure you have the most complete and accurate information possible.

## Checklist – Chapter Three

### Collect and Analyze Data

- ✓ Plan for maintaining confidentiality of individual data.
- ✓ Make sure the methods you select are suited to answering your evaluation questions.
- ✓ Assess individual and group-level change.
- ✓ Consider various methods of measuring change.
- ✓ If you have a large enough sample, conduct a pilot study.
- ✓ If you are using surveys, plan ahead for ensuring good response rates.
- ✓ Be mindful of issues regarding the measurement of change.
- ✓ Plan for data storage and treatment.
- ✓ Plan for data analysis.

# 4 CHAPTER FOUR
## Interpret and Communicate Evaluation Findings

Evaluations fail to live up to their full promise when what is learned is not appropriately communicated or goes unused. It's important that stakeholders understand the evaluation process doesn't end when all of the data have been collected, analyzed, and interpreted. On the contrary, this stage is the time to revisit the reasons the evaluation was originally commissioned. To ensure that your evaluation findings will be used to support learning, implement decisions, and make improvements, you need to communicate the results. Depending on your role, you may also be involved in identifying specific courses of action, developing a detailed action plan, and monitoring the action plan's implementation.

The activities we describe in this section create a greater likelihood that the evaluation recommendations will be carefully considered and translated into action and that the actions taken will be realistic and sensitive to the relevant cultures and contexts. These activities will also help stakeholders identify and manage any potential barriers or obstacles to change, and they will allow those individuals affected by the changes to get involved in planning the changes. Perhaps most importantly, these activities lay the groundwork for the stakeholders to use the evaluation findings as part of a continuous process of improvement and learning (Preskill & Torres, 1999). When consulting with stakeholders about findings, the purpose is not to change the findings but to discuss the findings and understand and integrate stakeholder perspectives. For instance, footnotes about actions that will be taken in response to negative findings may make it easier to communicate the negative findings and to point out that action is already being taken as a result of the evaluation. As you work through the communication needs, consider the following:

- Who needs to know?
- What do they need to know?
- Why do they need to know?
- How can they best know?
- When do they need to know?

## Include and Engage Stakeholders

Evaluations can result in a final report that is submitted to the primary stakeholder, client, or foundation. All too often, few people read that final report, so the degree of change that occurs as a result of the evaluation is limited. Evaluators can counter this tendency by carefully considering their interpretation and reporting strategy while keeping the goal of a usable evaluation in mind. Organizations will more often use evaluation reports that are credible, relevant (to stakeholders' interests, expectations, and communication preferences), accurate, and fair.

To effectively communicate, you will need to consider what needs to be communicated to whom and how you will distribute the information. Including and engaging stakeholders, as appropriate, throughout the process by distributing interim and draft reports before the release of a final report is a useful and effective sensemaking and communication tactic. This transparent and frequent communication enables you to better understand what information is helpful as well as see how different groups interpret and use data.

Developing and applying an evaluative rubric (described in Chapter Two) is one way to engage stakeholders in interpretation. You may have developed an evaluative rubric during the planning phase of the evaluation. If so, now is a good time to revisit, update, and apply the rubric. If you didn't previously create a rubric, it isn't too late. Although creating a rubric during the planning phase helps make stakeholder expectations explicit before data collection begins, introducing a rubric approach during the interpretation phase helps to make the interpretation within and across stakeholder groups transparent. Rubrics can be used to combine information from different sources to arrive at an evaluative judgment—for instance, is the program good enough to warrant continued investment? Developing a rubric can document what data were taken into account in making that judgment. In short, the rubric documents how evidence was used to arrive at an evaluative decision of "good" or "bad," or what needs improvement and what functions well.

Using more visual approaches for data sharing can help stakeholders understand data more quickly and engage with it more readily. See below for some tips on how to make your visualization effective.

## Exhibit 4.1 – Data Visualization Tips

Communicating with data visualization is increasingly commonplace and necessary for better understanding and use of evaluation. Pictures and graphs can be extremely valuable for communicating information quickly and easily to multiple audiences. Some suggestions for data visualizations include:

- Consider the elements of an effective visual, including
  - data density (the amount of data in a given space is not too overwhelming);
  - visual appeal (the balance of size, color, and shape of the visual); and
  - ease of understanding (the interpretability of the information presented).
- Try to understand the context and informational needs of your client group.
- Consider using software that you already use to produce pieces of powerful visuals. For example, you can expand your skills using presentation or spreadsheet applications.
- Use data labels and color but understand how and when to use them.
- Balance creativity with a simple and clean design.
- Isolation and color can be a great tool for stressing an important point or finding.

## Use Multiple and Targeted Communication Approaches

Evaluation results are not the final goal—moving toward improvement and impact are. To make sure the evaluation reaches people and that the information is acted upon, consider using multiple methods for communicating and reporting the process of the evaluation and its results. A broad communication strategy can help distribute the lessons arising from development initiatives and emphasize that the results of an evaluation provide information that can and should be used in an organizational-learning process. Informing a variety of audiences about the findings of the evaluation and how the results will be used increases the credibility of the evaluation effort, communicates to stakeholders that they were heard and that the results will be acted on, and prepares stakeholders for future evaluations by demonstrating their potential value. At a broad level, communication channels for evaluation information can include e-mail, web pages, face-to-face and virtual meetings, and paper-based collateral (flyers, posters, and so on). Some of the more specific approaches we use most often include:

- presentations with handouts (in person or virtual);
- executive briefings of key information;
- interactive dashboards of key data;
- illustrative case studies or vignettes;
- e-mail summaries of highlights and recommendations;
- videos of stakeholders talking about the importance, process, or impact of the initiative;
- infographics of key data and insights;

- photo essays that show the process or impact of the initiative; and
- town-hall-style meetings.

Tailoring and presenting information to effectively reach and inform stakeholders is critical. For example, high-level leaders and executives do not have time for or interest in a complete and detailed account of findings. They often want results and information that helps them make necessary changes or decisions. Finally, when a development initiative is designed to occur in stages or has separate components, evaluation reports can be issued at each stage as well as rolled up in a final, comprehensive report. We outline some of the basic elements of such a report in Exhibit 4.2.

## Tailoring the Report to Stakeholder Interests

Information about the stakeholder group's background, communication preferences, and information needs should be available from the initial planning phase of the evaluation; if it is not available, ask for it. What information do stakeholder groups want? When do they need or want the information? How do they best receive information? The most wonderful evaluation is not worth much if the key stakeholders do not know about it or understand how to make sense of or use the information. Strategically thinking about your communication approach will improve the likelihood that people are getting the information they need and can use it.

### Exhibit 4.2 – Basic Elements of a Final Evaluation Report

A final evaluation report should be clearly written and tailored specifically to its intended audience. Avoid words that may be unfamiliar to the intended audience, and, if you must use technical language (or jargon), explain it in layperson terms. Use graphs or narratives to illustrate a point. The report should be attractive and professional, and it should not be overwhelming; use headings and page numbers to help orient the reader. When appropriately used, color images, photographs, call-out boxes, and dashboards can add interest and clarity to the report. Do not neglect to pay attention to correct grammar, spelling, and punctuation. For organizing purposes, the list below can be a helpful guide.

The most useful evaluation reports provide both critical findings and recommended actions. Once you have identified these key elements of the report, you will want to make sure they stand out and are easily understood. The actions must be specific and follow logically from the evaluation results.

We recommend Stephanie Evergreen's book, *Effective Data Visualization*, as an excellent resource for how to organize an evaluation report so it is most useful and interesting to stakeholders (Evergreen, 2016). Although most evaluation reports include the following key elements, descriptions of the initiative and evaluation methods can often be included in appendices so the report focuses primarily on what the data tell us about the initiative.

- **Executive Summary:** Highlight the most important parts of the findings, including recommendations.
- **Purpose of the Evaluation:** Indicate why the evaluation was conducted, including the core evaluation questions and stakeholders.
- **Conclusions and Recommendations:** This section should be extremely clear so that your stakeholders know exactly what has occurred and what changes they may need to make.

*(continued)*

**Exhibit 4.2 – Basic Elements of a Final Evaluation Report (continued)**

- **Summary of Data (with multiple subsections):** The section could be divided by evaluation questions, by results related to the implementation of the initiative as opposed to the outcomes (short, mid, and long term) of the initiative, or by overall lessons learned. The organization of sections depends very much on what was examined by the evaluation, what was found, and what would be the most salient way to present them to your stakeholders.
- **Description of Initiative and Sample:** Include the title of the initiative and what the initiative sought to accomplish and who participated in it. Basic demographic information about participants can be helpful to include, as well as a description of the stakeholders from whom data were collected for the evaluation.
- **Overview of Processes Used and Analysis:** What data were collected, how, and when? Was there anything out of the ordinary about the methodology or processes used? Provide samples of your evaluation methodologies as appendices (for example, survey questions).
- **Limitations of the Evaluation:** Usually evaluators are not able to gather data from all stakeholder groups or all people within a stakeholder group. It is important to acknowledge what information or perspectives might be missing.
- **Appendices (supporting materials):** These can include more detail on methods used, a copy of data-collection tools, data-analysis tables (detailed), and other resources that are pertinent to understanding the report but may not be of interest to all readers.

## Checklist – Chapter Four

### Interpret and Communicate Evaluation Findings

- ✓ Draft the final evaluation report with key stakeholders in mind. Consider how best to inform and engage the stakeholders so the findings will be used to learn, make improvements, and increase impact.
- ✓ Include and engage stakeholders by asking for their feedback and input on draft reports and recommendations.
- ✓ Revisit and use your evaluative rubric to synthesize information from different sources and determine evaluative judgments.
- ✓ Use graphics and visual approaches to engage stakeholders and make it easy to understand data highlights.
- ✓ Use multiple and targeted communication approaches tailored to how stakeholders will best receive the information (for instance, one-page handout with summary of findings and recommendations, video summary, and PowerPoint).

5

# CHAPTER FIVE
## Implement Changes and Share Lessons Learned

Ultimately, evaluation findings need to be put to use, or else the resources and time that were invested in the evaluation were not used wisely. In some cases, it makes sense to use evaluation findings at the end of an initiative to guide future directions. In other cases, particularly in longer-term, more complex initiatives (for instance, leadership culture change), evaluation data can and should be used in every stage to test hypotheses about what is working to make progress toward desired outcomes and what is not.

One possible outcome of a leadership-development initiative is that it has the impact stakeholders and participants have expected and hoped for. In that case, no remedial action is necessary, but the organization might want to consider its next step in the development process and stakeholders may want to show off and celebrate the success of the initiative.

Another possible outcome is that the data show the initiative needs to be revised to achieve maximum impact. This is frequently the case for brand-new initiatives and should be viewed as part of the process rather than as a failure. In this case the specific areas and suggestions for revision, based on the evaluation findings, should be identified and prioritized by relevant stakeholder groups. For example, participants might gain insights but aren't able to employ much of what they learn because of systemic obstacles in their work environment or a lack of understanding about how to transfer what they've learned. Evaluators can help identify barriers, but it is the responsibility of an organization to address those issues.

Depending on the nature of the obstacles, additional development interventions may be needed. Sometimes the evaluation uncovers things that weren't previously known. For example, if the leadership-development initiative involved a culture or climate survey, the information gathered from the survey may indicate the work the organization needs to do. An organization may want to update reward systems, policies, or communication processes to better reflect the vision of the organization. Perhaps the leadership competencies being developed don't align with a business strategy, a community's values, or a foundation's culture.

It's best if stakeholders examine these issues before the leadership-development initiative, but sometimes that's not possible. Changes in other contextual factors may occur during the initiative or may not be readily apparent before the initiative starts. It's important to maintain attention on issues of alignment throughout the initiative to best ensure its success. Other experts, such as organizational-development professionals, may need to be consulted if there is a substantial incongruity among systems, processes, outcomes, and other factors.

## Gather and Consult with Stakeholders

The most effective means for determining how to use what is learned from the evaluation is to bring together everyone with a stake in the evaluation and the initiative. This includes not just participants and stakeholders with an interest in the development initiative but also people who might be affected by changes made as a result of the findings and those individuals responsible for implementing the intended changes. The best time to do this is after you've reported evaluation results, which allows stakeholders some time to think about the results and correct any misunderstandings or errors in the report. Stakeholders should be encouraged to use data to respond to any perceived inaccuracies in the report because this creates a shared responsibility for report accuracy.

If your evaluation results illustrate the shortcomings of a specific group in particular (such as the need for participants' managers to become better development coaches for their direct reports), it may be wise to allow that group time to devise a course of action before bringing in all the stakeholders. This time will allow the group to form a response and take ownership of the situation, instead of putting them in a defensive position.

## Examine Possible Revisions to the Initiative and to Specific Areas That Strengthen Support Structures

Evaluation findings might indicate a need for minor or major revision to the development initiative, such as including additional learning needs for individuals or groups and improving specific elements to support learning more broadly, thereby increasing an intervention's appeal or effect. Based on the evaluation findings, a group of stakeholders may assume the task of redesigning aspects of the initiative.

## Develop an Action Plan

Once key stakeholders have discussed potential actions, the next step is for them to develop an action plan. As an evaluator, you may or may not be involved in or lead the action-planning process. An action plan is a tool for implementing the lessons that result from an evaluation study.

Certainly, the lessons should point to areas of leadership-development initiatives that need revision, and in addition they can indicate areas (such as systems and processes) in the organization that aren't supporting those initiatives.

You can determine which stakeholders need to be involved in the action planning by examining where action is needed and who has the responsibility and authority to enact change in that area. The action plan should outline specific tasks, identify individuals who are responsible for carrying them out, include necessary resources for implementing specific actions, and provide a timeline for carrying them out. As a guide to creating an action-plan document, consider these questions:

- What needs to happen and why? What are the specific actions to be taken? How are the actions indicated by the evaluation results?
- Who will take action? What group or individual is responsible for implementing the proposed actions?
- Who else needs to be involved? What additional groups or individuals are needed (for example, to participate in the actions, to provide approval for them, or to play a support role)?
- What barriers are anticipated? What obstacles to implementation exist? How will obstacles be addressed?
- In what order do actions need to happen? Do the steps need to occur in a particular order?

- When does the action plan need to happen? Is there a deadline for initiating and completing each step of the action plan?
- How will the stakeholders know the action plan has happened? What indicators will be observed to determine whether each step of the action plan has been initiated and completed?
- How will success be determined? What indicators will be observed to measure the success of each step in the action plan?

The action plan that results from this effort needs to be distributed to everyone involved with the proposed actions so that all are clear about their roles in implementing the plan.

## Monitor the Action Plan's Implementation

As an action plan is implemented, its progress will need to be monitored and communicated. Depending on your role, you may be the person tasked with this effort. Monitoring the action plan's implementation means following up with individuals and groups responsible for specific actions, as indicated in the plan, to see how well they are progressing and what, if anything, needs to be modified. One way to monitor the plan is to periodically convene the group that developed the action plan and have each member describe how well the actions are being implemented and what help is needed to continue the process. Regardless of the method used, all of those involved should be aware of the extent to which the plan is being implemented and what impact the changes are having on individuals, groups, and the organization. The group might even decide that, as a result of making certain changes, additional evaluation needs have surfaced.

## Use Evaluation to Create Broader Change and Learning

Evaluation measures more than impact. The process has the potential to create change in (and for) individuals, organizations, and communities. In addition to identifying gaps in, barriers to, and support for leadership development, evaluation can be used to help gather possible solutions and solicit ideas for improving a development effort. These changes can affect broad or small groups of people or individuals, depending on the type of change and the effect it has at various levels. These changes also provide an opportunity for additional evaluation and learning.

Important outcomes of evaluation include the individual and group learning that occurs as a result of participating in the evaluation and using its results. When individuals and groups reflect upon their experiences and share what they've learned with others in the organization, the organization as a whole learns. The challenge, however, is in finding ways to capture and share this learning.

One tactic is to develop a learning database that employees and other stakeholders can access on an as-needed basis. Another tactic is to create online discussion groups or communities of practice for groups within the organization. Yet another is to publish, in internal or external newsletters and bulletins, the lessons revealed through participation in the development initiative and in the evaluation's results. Each of these methods is a vehicle for sharing information more broadly so that people and groups can learn from each other—a hallmark of learning. In creating an evaluation plan that fosters learning, it's important to consider guidelines that make the process less susceptible to misuse. The collection, storage, and use of data representing individuals should adhere to appropriate and professional standards (Yarbrough, Shulha, Hopson, & Caruthers, 2011). Following these various standards helps reduce ethical problems that can arise during the evaluation process.

Three specific issues are especially relevant to the evaluation of leadership-development initiatives: maintaining confidentiality of individual data; evaluating the initiative, not the individuals; and linking the evaluation to broader goals and strategies. The evaluation data collected should be used to enhance the initiative itself, to foster changes in participants' leadership knowledge and skills, to encourage relevant changes in the organization or community, and to illustrate relevant factors in the organization or community related to the success of the initiative. Evaluators should encourage organizations not to use the collected data for performance appraisals or for administrative decisions about individual performance, since the collection of that kind of information is held to a different set of legal and professional standards (Yarbrough et al., 2011). You can promote this value by aggregating any individual data collected during the evaluation to the group level.

Evaluation should be part of strategic intent. It should not be a valueless exercise that people contribute their time, energy, and resources to but has no productive purpose. Just as leadership development should be linked to organizational strategy, so should evaluation be considered strategically important and expected to contribute to the achievement of goals and learning agendas.

## Checklist – Chapter Five

### Implement Changes and Share Lessons Learned

- ✓ Gather and consult with stakeholders to determine how to use what was learned from the evaluation.
- ✓ Examine possible revisions to the initiative and to specific areas that strengthen support structures.
- ✓ Explore the need to provide follow-up support for the leadership-development initiative.
- ✓ Suggest and possibly help develop a detailed action plan.
- ✓ Suggest and possibly help create a process for monitoring the action plan's implementation.
- ✓ Use evaluation to create broader change and learning.

# CHAPTER SIX
## Emerging Issues, Trends, and Future Directions

In the introduction of this book we mentioned that leadership, leadership development, and evaluation are all evolving. Throughout we have shared our current thoughts and practices on evaluating leadership development. We want to end the book by sharing emerging issues and trends that have a direct impact on how we develop leadership and how we conduct evaluations.

Our definition and understanding of leadership is regularly evolving. A growing body of work is focusing on *leadership as a networked process* (Meehan & Reinelt, 2014). Understanding networks and incorporating the development of networks into leadership development has a clear impact on how we evaluate outcomes. For example, outcomes of leadership-development efforts may increasingly include improving individuals' abilities to understand and leverage the existing network as well as building networks within teams, across parts of an organization, and between organizations. We included information on using network analysis in Chapter Three because this analysis is more frequently used as a method for assessing changes in organizational networks as a result of leadership development that aims to improve collaboration, the exchange of innovative ideas, and the leadership capacity within organizations. More work is needed to understand the links between specific development initiatives, changes in network structure and composition, and outcomes associated with stronger networks.

We are also seeing more of a shift from individual skill-building (or competency development) to what is called *vertical development*: helping individuals develop more complex and sophisticated ways of thinking (Petrie, 2014). This focus on changing mindsets is considered critical to leading in a complex, interconnected, and rapidly changing world. The concept of vertical development of individuals has also been applied to describe organizational-leadership cultures (McCauley, Palus, Drath, Hughes, McGuire, O'Connor, & Van Velsor, 2008; McGuire & Rhodes, 2009). Understanding the impact of this type of development presents clear challenges for identifying measurable outcomes and effective evaluation. How do we efficiently assess various stages of vertical development in individuals and organizations, as well as the impact that this type of development has on leadership outcomes? Some measures do exist to assess individuals and teams, but they have not yet been used widely in evaluation of leadership development.

CCL has a long history of acknowledging the importance of experience-driven development; the book by McCauley, Derue, Yostt, and Taylor (2013) describes how to foster on-the-job development. There are more and more virtual-learning opportunities, personalized leadership coaching, and development experiences that do not occur at work or in a training room; these might include learning about leadership while driving a race car or working with horses. Learning and development can occur in short bursts of development over different time frames and at the discretion of the learner. This self-paced, tailored, and self-directed learning can be powerful, and it creates new opportunities to collect evaluation data as part of the learning process and challenges since the initiative is not consistent across people or time.

There is increasing recognition of the importance of being culturally responsive in leadership development and in evaluation, and there are more guidance and tools for doing that well, though there is more work to be done. At a minimum, global leadership-development initiatives require you to consider collecting data in different languages and employing techniques to understand potential differences in how people respond and rate their experiences and what they need to best apply what they learn. At a deeper level, it ramps up the need to attend to assumptions, understand norms and expectations, and explore the possible interpretations and consequences of processes and actions. For example, what may seem like an insignificant finding in one context could be deeply threatening in another.

There are new tools and sources for data collection such as social media, phone apps, pulse surveys, and self-monitoring technologies that provide opportunities to capture real-time feedback and possibly more accurate measures of things like the frequency of certain behaviors or responses to certain people or situations. Data systems are increasingly used by organizations to connect their performance with industry benchmarks and to provide tools for analyzing organizational data with other data sources. Big Data and human-capital analytics are leading us all to think more in terms of data-collection systems and standardizing data collection, which could lead to more rigorous and empirical benchmarks for leadership-development evaluation, if we are thoughtful about how we approach it.

Evaluation is often a complex endeavor, and it may become more complex as a result of these and other developing trends. It is impossible for any single book to provide all the information that may be needed for a particular situation. Our goal has been to provide an overview of the evaluative process with examples of techniques, strategies, and guidelines that you can use to ensure that your evaluation is meaningful, useful, and credible. In addition, following our guidance, you can make sure your evaluation is not an isolated process. By linking your evaluation to the design and results of development initiatives and to broader goals, you can help build systems and processes that augment the individual and group impact of leadership development.

# REFERENCES

American Evaluation Association. (2011). *Public Statement on Cultural Competence in Evaluation*. Fairhaven, MA: Author. Retrieved from www.eval.org

Bersin, J. (2006). *High-impact learning measurement: Best practices, models, and business-driven solutions for the measurement and evaluation of corporate training*. Oakland, CA: Bersin & Associates.

Cullen, K., Palus, C., & Appaneal, C. (2013). *Developing network perspective. Understanding the basics of social networks and their role in leadership* (CCL White Paper). Greensboro, NC: Center for Creative Leadership.

Davidson, E. J. (2005). *Evaluation methodology basics: The nuts and bolts of sound evaluation*. Thousand Oaks, CA: Sage.

Davies, R., & Dart, J. (2005). *The most significant change (MSC) technique: A guide to its use*. Retrieved from www.mande.co.uk/docs/MSCGuide.htm

Evergreen, S. D. H. (2016). *Effective data visualization: The right chart for the right data*. Thousand Oaks, CA: Sage.

Fredericks, K., & Carman, J. (2013). *Using social network analysis in evaluation. A report to the Robert Wood Johnson Foundation*. Retrieved from http://rwjf.org/en/research-publications/find-rwjfresearch/2013/12/using-social-network-analysis-in-evaluation.html

Gamble, J. (2008). *A developmental evaluation primer*. Montreal, Quebec: The J.W. McConnell Family Foundation.

Greenbaum, T. L. (1999). *Moderating focus groups: A practical guide for group facilitation*. Thousand Oaks, CA: Sage.

Hannum, K. M., & Martineau, J. W. (2008). *Evaluating the impact of leadership development*. San Francisco, CA: Pfeiffer.

Hannum, K. M., Martineau, J. W., & Reinelt, C. (Eds.). (2007). *The handbook of leadership development evaluation*. San Francisco, CA: Jossey-Bass.

Hoole, E., & Martineau, J. W. (2014). Evaluation methods. In D. V. Day, (Ed.), *The Oxford handbook of leadership and organizations* (pp. 167–198). New York, NY: Oxford University Press.

Hoppe, B., & Reinelt, C. (2010). Social network analysis and the evaluation of leadership networks. *The Leadership Quarterly, 21,* 600–619.

Inouye, T., Cao Yu, H., & Adefuin, J. (2005, January). *Commissioning multicultural evaluation: A foundation resource guide.* Oakland, CA: The California Endowment's Diversity in Health Education Project (Report published in partnership with Social Policy Research Associates).

Kirkpatrick, D. L., & Kirkpatrick, J. D. (2014). *Evaluating training programs: The four levels* (3rd ed.). San Francisco, CA: Berrett-Koehler.

Krebs, V., & Holley, J. (2006). *Building smart communities through network weaving.* Athens, OH: Appalachian Center for Economic Networks.

Marsden, P. V. (1990). Network data and measurement. *Annual Review of Sociology*, Volume 16, pp. 435–463.

Martineau, J. W., & Patterson, T. E. (2010). Evaluating leader development. In E. Van Velsor, C. D. McCauley, & M. N. Ruderman (Eds.), *The Center for Creative Leadership handbook of leadership development* (3rd ed., pp. 251–281). San Francisco, CA: Jossey-Bass.

McCauley, C. D., Palus, C. J., Drath, W. H., Hughes, R. L., McGuire, J. B, O'Connor, P. M. G., & Van Velsor, E. (2008). *Interdependent leadership in organizations: Evidence from six case studies* (CCL Research Report no. 190). Greensboro, NC: Center for Creative Leadership.

McCauley, C., Derue, D., Yostt, P., & Taylor, S. (2013). *Experience-driven leader development: Models, tools, best practices, and advice for on-the-job development.* San Francisco, CA: Wiley.

McGuire, J. B., & Rhodes, G. (2009). *Transforming your leadership culture.* San Francisco, CA: Jossey-Bass.

Meehan, D., & Reinelt, C. (2014). *Leadership and networks: New ways of developing leadership in a highly connected world. Oakland, CA: Leadership Learning Community.* (Report funded by the Annie E. Casey Foundation and the David and Lucile Packard Foundation.) Retrieved from http://leadershiplearning.org/system/files/LLCNetworkNLfinal4.pdf

Mehta, S., & Downs, H. (2016). *Six strategies for digital learning success* (CCL White Paper). Greensboro, NC: Center for Creative Leadership.

Morgan, D. L. (1993). *Successful focus groups: Advancing the state of the art.* Thousand Oaks, CA: Sage.

Morgan, D. L., & Krueger, R. A. (1997). *The focus group kit* (vols. 1–6). Thousand Oaks, CA: Sage.

Patton, M. Q. (2011). *Developmental evaluation: Applying complexity concepts to enhance innovation and use.* New York, NY: The Guilford Press.

Peterson, D. B. (1993). *Measuring change: A psychometric approach to evaluating individual training outcomes.* Paper presented at the eighth annual conference of the Society for Industrial and Organizational Psychology, San Francisco, CA.

Petrie, N. (2014). *Vertical leadership development—part 1: Developing leaders for a complex world* (CCL White Paper). Greensboro, NC: Center for Creative Leadership.

Philips J. J., Phillips P., & Ray, R. (2012). *Measuring leadership development: Quantify your program's impact and ROI on organizational performance.* McGraw-Hill.

Preskill, H., & Russ-Eft, D. (2015). *Building evaluation capacity: 72 activities for teaching and training* (2nd ed.). Thousand Oaks, CA: Sage.

Preskill, H., & Torres, R. T. (1999). *Evaluative inquiry for learning in organizations.* Thousand Oaks, CA: Sage.

Yarbrough, D. B., Shulha, L. M., Hopson, R. K., & Caruthers, F. A. (2011). *The program evaluation standards: A guide for evaluators and evaluation users* (3rd ed.). Thousand Oaks, CA: Sage.

# ABOUT THE AUTHORS

**Tracy E. Patterson** is director of the Center for Creative Leadership's Evaluation Center, which supports CCL by expanding knowledge, methods, and approaches related to the evaluation of leadership development. She holds a master's degree in public policy from Duke University.

**Sarah Stawiski** is a senior research associate at the Center for Creative Leadership. She specializes in designing and conducting evaluations of programs focused on developing individual leaders and improving organizations' collective leadership capabilities. She holds a Ph.D. in social psychology from Loyola University Chicago.

**Kelly M. Hannum** is president of Aligned Impact LLC and an adjunct staff member for the Center for Creative Leadership. She holds a Ph.D. in educational research, measurement, and evaluation from the University of North Carolina at Greensboro.

**Heather Champion** is manager of Client Evaluation Services at the Center for Creative Leadership. She works with a range of global clients and partners to design and conduct customized evaluations to assess the impact of CCL leadership solutions, programs, products, and services. She holds a Ph.D. in developmental psychology from North Carolina State University,

**Holly Downs** is a senior evaluation faculty member at the Center for Creative Leadership and is the principal investigator for CCL's Virtual Leadership Learning Project. Her experience in research and evaluation has emphasized studying programs delivered in traditional, hybrid, and digital learning environments to myriad audiences. She holds a Ph.D. in educational psychology from the University of Illinois at Urbana-Champaign.

# ABOUT THE CENTER FOR CREATIVE LEADERSHIP

The Center for Creative Leadership (CCL®) is a top-ranked, global provider of leadership development. By leveraging the power of leadership to drive results that matter most to clients, CCL transforms individual leaders, teams, organizations, and society. Its array of cutting-edge solutions is steeped in extensive research and experience gained from working with hundreds of thousands of leaders at all levels. Ranked among the world's top five providers of executive education by the *Financial Times* and in the Top 10 by *Bloomberg BusinessWeek*, CCL has offices in Greensboro, NC; Colorado Springs, CO; San Diego, CA; Brussels, Belgium; Moscow, Russia; Addis Ababa, Ethiopia; Johannesburg, South Africa; Singapore; Gurgaon, India; and Shanghai, China.

CPSIA information can be obtained
at www.ICGtesting.com
Printed in the USA
FSOW03n0113310517
34634FS